From the Library of

Andrew Bosarge

The ROUND-UP

-A-
PICTORIAL
HISTORY
-of-
WESTERN
Movie & Televison
STARS
Through The Years!

COMPILED AND EDITED BY

DONALD R. KEY

Other Western movie books published by Empire Publishing, Inc:

The Roy Rogers Reference-Trivia-Scrapbook Book by David Rothel
The Gene Autry Reference-Trivia-Scrapbook Book by David Rothel
More Cowboy Shooting Stars by John A. Rutherford and Richard B. Smith, III
Allan "Rocky" Lane, Republic's Action Ace by Chuck Thornton and David Rothel
Tom Mix Highlights by Andy Woytowich
An Ambush of Ghosts by David Rothel
Tim Holt by David Rothel
Whatever Happened to Randolph Scott? by C. H. Scott
Randolph Scott / A Film Biography by Jefferson Brim Crow, III
Saddle Gals by Steve Turner and Edgar M. Wyatt

Empire Publishing, Inc.
Box 717
Madison, NC 27025-0717
(910) 427-5850

The Round-Up © 1995 by Donald R. Key

Library of Congress Catalog Number 93-74258
ISBN Number 0-944019-12-9

Published and printed in the United States of America

1 2 3 4 5 6 7 8 9 0

FRONT COVER: Monte Hale
BACK COVER: Roy Rogers

To all the
Ladies and Gentlemen
Who Gave Us
Endless Hours of Excitement and Pleasure,
this Pictorial/Encyclopedia/History Book
Is Proudly Dedicated.

CONTENTS

A WORD FROM THE PUBLISHER

Over the years, we at Empire Publishing have been directly involved in the fascinating world of publishing books and publications about movies and the people involved in making movies. In 1974 we created and first published a monthly movie collector's newspaper entitled *The Big Reel*. As owners and operators, we continued publishing it for twenty years. In the field of book publishing we have centered our interest directly on books about movie stars of the western genre. We have published books on Gene Autry, Roy Rogers, Lash LaRue, Iron Eyes Cody, Tim Holt, Randolph Scott, Rocky Lane and others. Although none of these books have produced earth-shattering sales, we have experienced complete satisfaction with publishing those books as we have interest in that era of movies which still produce fond memories for us.

With the publishing of this book we have taken a different look than that of all other cowboy books. Fans often ask us, "What book has *all* the cowboy stars?" Of course, we did not have such a book available. . . until now. In your hands is a western movie encyclopedia, pictorial and history book which we have titled *The Round-Up*. We have made an effort to "round-up" more than 300 cowboy heroes, heroines, character actors, sidekicks, and even villains who have been a part of making western movies from the turn of the century through the 1990s. It contains 300+ full page photographs on top-quality glossy stock paper and is bound in hardcover for years of enjoyment. It is our belief that if you only buy one western book in your lifetime, *The Round-Up* is definitely the one for you to acquire.

When the idea to produce this book came about, it was our desire to "round-up" and feature as many actors as was reasonably possible. However, as the number of western movie actors and actresses who have appeared in pictures since the turn of the century would number in the thousands, we definitely did *not* include them all. To include them all would have been impossible for us as the book would need to contain hundreds more pages and the printing cost would probably prohibit us from producing the book at all. The selection of whom to include was solely the decision of the publisher. Some actors were chosen due to their popularity; some were included because of the availability of good photos; and some were included because they are personal favorites of the publisher. Therefore, when you look through *The Round-Up* pictorial, although you may realize that some of *your* favorite western movie actors may not be included, we ask that you not be critical of any omissions, but instead, we suggest that you appreciate and enjoy the ones that *are* represented here.

As the birthdates on movie celebrities have been altered through the years in many cases, we found that it is impossible to give factual dates on some. Therefore we have gone to our expert researchers, and to the best of their and our knowledge and research ability, we are in agreement that the dates in this book are as accurate as possible. We are sure, despite all efforts, that there are some errors contained in this book; however, we all have confidence that we have done our best to keep the dates and other information factual.

In closing, we would like to share a few memorable thoughts that perhaps will bring back some happy times and jolly moments to you:

A wonderful thing used to happen on Saturdays about 50 years ago. I would go to the local movie house, pay my dime, and enter into a world of adventure. The theatre lights became dim and the show would begin: first a couple of cartoons; then the serial chapter; and next, the exciting highlight of the day — the western.

The western film was a world of its own. For approximately 60 minutes, I was totally involved with the cowboy star as he corraled outlaws either pulling off stagecoach and bank holdups, plotting to drive out homesteaders, stirring up range wars to acquire all the land in a particular valley for its valuable water rights, jumping miners' claims for gold or silver deposits, or staving off Indian attacks.

For more that 50 years, some of my best friends have been cowboys. Ken Maynard, John Wayne, Tex Ritter, Allan "Rocky" Lane, and Wild Bill Elliott were intimate acquaintances of mine. Sunset Carson, Tim Holt, Monte Hale, Lash LaRue, Rod Cameron, and The Durango Kid were as real to me as my own family. I knew them all. As a youngster, I loved those westerns, and even as a grown up, I still do. I have fond memories of sitting around the campfires with my heroes during a cattle drive. In those days I rode shotgun for Rex Allen; the Wild West was a wonderful place to be. Cinema saddle sores (from watching and riding through the same Saturday matinee three times) and dust in my tired eyes (from sitting too near the screen) were only a couple of pleasures I enjoyed as I was entertained hour after hour.

If you are like me, past 50, or will admit to 60, or even a young 70, you will remember those exciting cowboy movies of yesteryear. Even if you are a youngster, or 20 or 30, names like Roy Rogers, Gene Autry, Johnny Mack Brown, and Hopalong Cassidy are familiar to you.

I would like to take this opportunity to invite you to sit back, relax and once again relive those by-gone days of the movie cowboy as you peruse The Round-Up.

8

ACKNOWLEDGMENTS

A publishing effort such as *The Round-Up* requires the talents and knowledge of many persons. To assure ourselves that the information contained within is as accurate as possible, we have searched out persons who are known to be very knowledgeable to assist us in the research for this book. It required the talents, time, and knowledge of many and we give our sincere thanks to all involved in this project.

For their many hours of research and dedication to the history and knowledge of western movies, we acknowledge the following western film enthusiasts and give them our grateful thanks. Our special appreciation goes to the following:

Bobby Copeland
Boyd Magers
Bill McDowell
John Rutherford
Clay Satcher
Richard B. Smith, III
Edgar M. Wyatt.

Without these individuals and others who assisted, this publication could not have been a factual record. We would also like to express our thanks to the following for helping to make this publication a reality:

Allan Barbour
Ronald Butler
Jerry Campbell
William C. Cline
Ray Courts
Sharon Courts
Mario DeMarco
Sammy Fulp
Peggy Gentry
Ken Griffis

Monte Hale
Joanne Hale
Milo Holt
James Howard
Ed Hulse
Ken D. Jones
Doneen Key
Noreen Key
Rhonda Lemons
Boyd Magers

Nick Matseas
Arthur McClure
David Rothel
Jim Shoenberger
Wayne Short
Harold Smith
Packy Smith
O. J. Sikes
Neil Summers
Steve Turner

THE WESTERN FILM — PAST AND PRESENT
by Ronald C. Butler

The early Western movies have been referred to over the years as B-Westerns, due to the low budget allowed to produce the pictures.

Some folks have said that B-Westerns were simply a novelty, a tasteless fad, with no real substance or significance. Others have said they were all quick-draw and make-believe, with only a casual glance at Wild-West reality. Still others have said that they were made quickly, cheaply, and much of the time not very well.

To all these folks, the B in B-Westerns stood for budget (low) and for B class and for bad. No doubt there is some degree of truth in all these characterizations. However, when one of these movies did have the brand of talent stamped upon it, no other type of film could be more enjoyable.

The B-Western was (and continues to be) a unique American paradox. While they may seem to be incredibly void of substance, yet to those who experienced them, they provided excitement and action that enlivened a thousand Saturday afternoons.

Kids and adults alike could not get enough of them.
The mountains and canyons and prairies.
The Indians, the cavalry, and the horses.
The thrill of the showdown, the shootout, and the punch-up.
The villain with the revealing smile and the thin-mustache.
The bush-whackers, the desperadoes, and the crooked bank presidents.
The cattle barons, the rustlers, and the claim-jumpers.
The double-dealing, back-shooting, two-timing, yellow-bellied, side winders.
The dirty varmints.
The bad-guys in black hats.
The nesters, the sheepherders, and the homesteaders all paunchy and righteousness.
The good guy.
The cowboy-hero, galloping across the screen 20 feet tall.
The one who put things right, who rode like the wind, and fought like a mountain lion.

While they may seem to be all quick-draw and make-believe, they had a special charm and value as an escape from the common and ordinary which, in most cases, more than compensated for their inadequacies. B-Westerns were not inferior films, they were very special films.

Wild West reality was never intended, but a Wild West of unreality that was better and certainly more fun was indeed deliberate. Who cared if the West wasn't really like that?

The 1930s and 40s were disruptive and grim decades for the average American. The Great Depression and World War II signified stressful times. Life was full of paradoxes and incongruities.

It took still another paradox, the B-Western, to make a positive impact. In those bleak years people wanted to look away from grim realities of failure, bankruptcy, foreclosure, knuckle-scraping poverty, and hungry ugliness. They looked to Hollywood to show good guys winning, to let them see heroes and pretty girls. And when they could spare a dime, they spent it at the movies. And the B-Western movies with their cowboy-heroes were the best bet.

The emotional conditioning provided by these films and the durability of that conditioning should never be underestimated. While B-Westerns certainly did not save the national character from collapse, they were important parts of many lives, sustaining many of their "faiths" by identifying with many powerful and admirable symbols of straight-forward righteousness.

The popularity of the B-Western was an extension of the cowboy myth in American life. The wild west tale with its miracle riding cowboy-hero is the American Myth — The National Fairy Tale. It is about a world that never really was but ought to have been, is not now but should be. It is the frontier experience transformed into something glorious and fantastic and romantic. It is The Great American Adventure characterized by historical fact and far-out fantasy, where the ultimate truth meets ultimate doubt and beats it to the draw.

It was a "useful myth," and it really did not matter that it wasn't accurate at all. The cowboy-hero received adoration and loyalty of amazing proportions, while villains were hissed at with equal fervor. Millions of kids throughout the United States fantasized being one or more of these Saturday afternoon heroes: Tom Mix, Hoot Gibson, Ken Maynard, Tim McCoy, Gene Autry, Dale Evans, Roy Rogers, Lash LaRue, Durango Kid, Buck Jones, Hopalong Cassidy, Wild Bill Elliott, Sunset Carson, etc.

They were indeed cowboy-movie-heroes — not actors who appeared in alternate movies as an Air Force officer, a Philadelphia lawyer, a cop, or as Doris Day's boyfriend. They were not James Stewart, Henry Fonda, Gregory Peck, Gary Cooper, Burt Lancaster, or Kirk Douglas. They were cowboy-heroes every single time they rode across the silver screen.

What other type of hero could shoot a gun from an outlaw's hand even though he appeared to be aiming his gun somewhere in the vicinity of the lowest hanging cloud?

What other type of hero could land a haymaker on the chin of a crook, and no matter if he seemed to miss the bad guy's chin by about five feet?

Where could you find a hero who never kissed the rancher's daughter even once or who could shoot 47 rounds from his six-gun without reloading or who never got his hat knocked off in a brawling fight?

Violence you say? Oh no! It was always understood that no one got hurt or killed. In our imaginations we could almost see them get up and walk away after being shot dead or being pulled from a flying horse.

Yes. B-Westerns were a Wild West of unreality; they were quick-draw and make-believe and cheaply made; and their story lines were straight-forward and uncomplicated with minimum dialogue. But this was a part of their appeal; this was what made them special!

Some folks like A-Westerns better than B-Westerns. One thing for sure — A's were certainly not B's. In the A category were such classics as *Red River, The Ox-Bow Incident, Duel in the Sun, One-Eyed Jacks, High Noon*, and *The Wild Bunch*. These films which emphasized reality and were costly to make were meant to be taken seriously. But they were not exactly what you would call cowboy-hero stuff. Front-row kids could not even see them without a letter from mother swearing they were a lot older than they looked.

The A's were a new kind of western movie — bigger and slower. And there was a new cowboy-puzzled, neurotic, and a little unsure of his position, who more often than not, rode into town, not as a knight but as an object of suspicion and mistrust. He did not gallop across the plains in search of wrongs that needed righting. And it wasn't so much the "code of the West" that inspired him to fight at the jangle of a spur.

Mostly, he rode around the wide open spaces in search of his own identity and fought only to achieve it or maintain it. It was a question of survival in a world he never made, but it was the only one he knew. His violence was awesome, but strictly personal and often he was its victim, dying right along with the bad guy. He was still, of course, a man of honor, and his word was as unbeatable as the quick-draw.

But he was not a boy scout. When he went into the saloon, he drank whiskey instead of milk and sarsaparilla. And sometimes he became staggering drunk, and his dignity took a battering although his integrity could never be doubted. His shirt was often more dusty than fancy. His stetson, if it was white, was no longer the simple symbol of moral purity. Battered and sweaty, it was merely something to keep the sun out of his eyes, or something in which to water his horse (a horse with no name).

The new cowboy-hero could be ruthless, violent, cruel, selfish, and unsportsmanlike, taking advantage whenever and however he could. But he was still tall in the saddle, even though he rode with confusion and contradiction.

Yes indeed, the B's were a lot different from the A's. To thousands upon thousands the B stood not for B class or bad; rather it stood for better, for best, for boom, but rarely for boring. To the producers who could turn out a B-Western in a week's time for $10,000 and be almost certain to bring in $50,000 in rental fees, the B stood for butter and bread and for bonanza and bucks.

Eventually, however, the B stood for Boot Hill. The Republic Eagle, the MGM Lion, the Columbia Torchbearer — all turned into dinosaurs. The end had come; it was 1952 and TV had the country by the eyeballs.

Everybody has his "fantasy place." This place, wherever it is, is an idea in one's mind; a kind of soul place through which you can keep in touch with personal make-believe; and a haven to dream your daydreams. Because this is true there will always be an audience for B-Westerns.

"What is a B-Western, you ask?" Well, there is one thing for sure — you will never understand fully until these memorable B Western phrases have unforgettable meaning:

> "They went thataway!"
> "Let's get outta here!"
> "Oh, the thrill of it all!"
> "So long, Rough Rider!"

MONTE HALE

In 1946 Monte Hale made his screen debut in Republic's first color Western, *Home on the Range*. With guitar in hand, he rode and sang his way through film after film and became a popular favorite at theaters everywhere. In 1956 Hale was awarded a role in the classic film *Giant* with James Dean. (1921-   )

FOREWORD
by Monte Hale

When I was a kid, it wasn't easy to get the ten cents for admission to the Saturday movie matinee. I loved to see Hoot Gibson, Tom Mix, and Ken Maynard features, along with following the hero week after week in serials such as William Desmond's *The Mysterious Rider*. If there was any money left, it would have been great to buy popcorn, but I always wound up in the lobby just smelling it while the kernels popped in the machine.

I was so fascinated with the picture show that I even enjoyed the ads and coming attractions. I can remember when I didn't have a dime and talking the manager into letting me sweep the sidewalks for an admission ticket. I never dreamed that someday I would be in show business, not even after I bought my first guitar, learned a few chords, and began singing in church and other places.

Later, I learned all the up-to-date songs, including one of my favorites, "San Antonio Rose." By then I was invited to Houston for an audition at The Ranch Club. They liked me, and I stayed there for five months! This was in the early 1940s, and soon afterwards I was able to land another opportunity to perform at a theater in Galveston. Although I couldn't afford it, I stayed at Galveston's Jean Lafitte Hotel, using the money I received for my appearances to pay the bill, and leaving little left over to survive.

Fortunately, one day between shows, I was in the lobby and met a gentleman by the name of Phil Isley (he was Jennifer Jones' father). He approached me and said, "Is this your guitar?" "Yes sir," I responded. He then asked me if I would like to join twenty-eight stars from Hollywood on a war bond drive. When he told me that Johnny Mack Brown, Gale Storm, Huntz Hall, Jimmy Wakely, and Chill Wills were just part of the lineup. I was ready to go right then and there. They needed a guitar player to accompany Lee "Lasses" White, and even though I knew I would not be paid, it seemed like a great opportunity.

As luck would have it, Phil sent a telegram about me to Herbert J. Yates, the kingpin at Republic Pictures in those days. This prompted a reply from the studio with an invitation to come to California for a screen test. I made my way to Hollywood, tested, and was pleased to receive a seven-year contract. They even told me that I would make my debut in Republic's first color Western, *Home on the Range* (1946).

While this was great news, the most memorable part of my days at Republic was the opportunity to meet and become friends with a great group of people. Some of my best buddies were Roy Barcroft (who almost always played a heavy but in real life was a fine gentleman), Bobby Blake, a young man with big talent, and lovely Adrian Booth, a dear lady who worked with me in several pictures. Many of my pardners and co-workers are here in *The Round-Up*. This book brings back many memories for me as I look through its pages and makes me think back to those days at Republic, just like my regular breakfast get-togethers with my dear friend Gene Autry do, when we reminisce about old times and all the great people we worked with over the years.

While I hung up my guitar and put aside scripts some time back, I still love to share my enthusiasm for the West with people. That's why today you can find me around the Autry Museum of Western Heritage, where my wife, Joanne, is chief executive officer and director. You'll often find me there shaking hands with folks from all over the world.

I would like to close with these thoughts:

> *Life is like a journey,*
> *Taken on a train*
> *With a pair of travelers at each window pane.*
> *I may sit beside you the whole journey through,*
> *Or I may sit elsewhere, never knowing you.*
> *But if fate should mark us to sit here side by side,*
> *Let's be pleasant travelers, because it's such a short ride.*

Shoot Low; They Might Be Crawlin'

Monte Hale
Studio City, California
August 1995

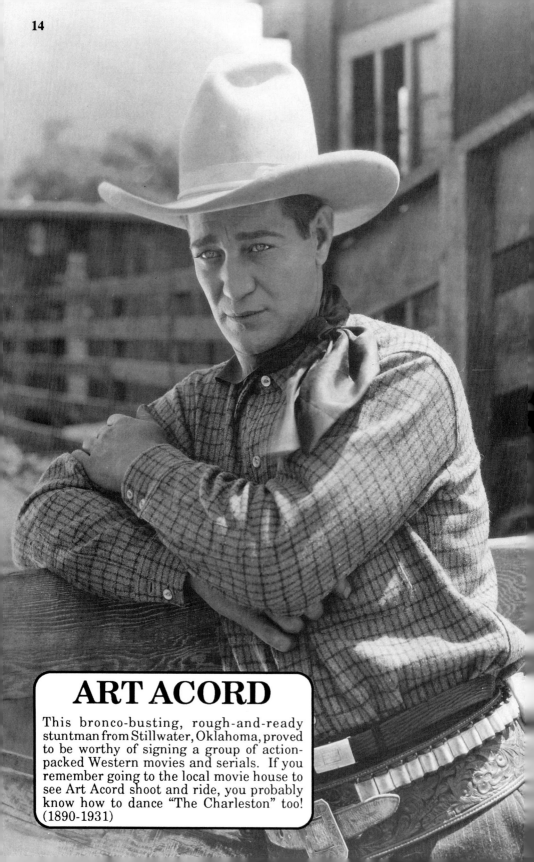

ART ACORD

This bronco-busting, rough-and-ready stuntman from Stillwater, Oklahoma, proved to be worthy of signing a group of action-packed Western movies and serials. If you remember going to the local movie house to see Art Acord shoot and ride, you probably know how to dance "The Charleston" too! (1890-1931)

ERNIE ADAMS

Ernie Adams' face frequently popped up in Westerns. He could be seen as a saloon keeper, running with cattle rustlers and bank robbers, and even on the side of the law. Adams' acting really excelled when he was cast as a "stoolie." (1885-1957)

TED ADAMS

Born in a theatre dressing room to perform-ing stage parents, Ted Adams later became a stage performer himself. That vocation led him to Hollywood where he was "hissed and booed" for his performances as villains in more than 100 pictures and seven serials. (1890-1973)

KAY ALDRIDGE

This glamorous actress retired from the screen in the mid-1940s, after having appeared in several chapter plays and a string of feature films. She was also a leading model, appearing on the cover of numerous magazines. (1917-1995)

BOB ALLEN

During the period 1935-1937, Bob Allen starred in his own series for Columbia Studios. He returned to the east coast in 1940 to pursue a career in stage acting and the real estate business. While appearing at several film-fan conventions during recent years, he wore his original movie outfit from the early days. (It still fit, too!) (1906-   )

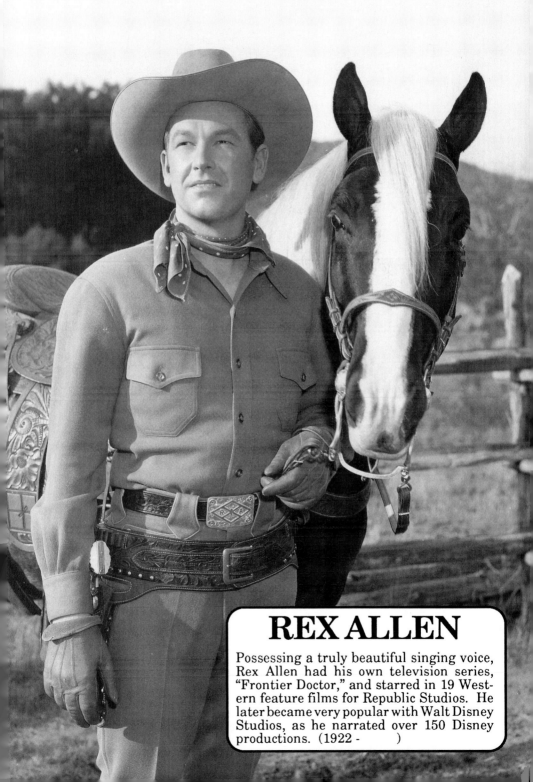

REX ALLEN

Possessing a truly beautiful singing voice, Rex Allen had his own television series, "Frontier Doctor," and starred in 19 Western feature films for Republic Studios. He later became very popular with Walt Disney Studios, as he narrated over 150 Disney productions. (1922 -   )

GILBERT "BRONCHO BILLY"ANDERSON

The first Western film, *The Great Train Robbery* produced by the Thomas Edison Company, was made in 1903, and Broncho Billy was among its cast members. Anderson retired in 1920 with a total of more than 400 films to his credit. (1884-1971)

LLOYD "ARKANSAS SLIM" ANDREWS

An unforgettable sidekick, comedian, and musician, Slim provided comedy for Tex Ritter, Don Barry, and Tom Keene pictures. He loved kids and spent the latter part of his career starring in a daily kids' television program. (1906-1992)

STANLEY ANDREWS

Although his film career spanned many years, Stanley Andrews is probably best known as The Old Ranger, narrator of the "Death Valley Days" television series. His character in that series spinned stories of the old West as it was really supposed to be. (1891-1969)

MORRIS ANKRUM

With a law degree in hand, Morris Ankrum became a real menace to such sagebrush heroes as Hopalong Cassidy. This "bad guy" appeared in nearly 150 features. (1897-1964)

JAMES ARNESS

TV's "Gunsmoke" was home base for James Arness from 1955-1975, as he portrayed Dodge City's famous marshal, Matt Dillon. Arness is the brother of another fine actor, Peter Graves. (1923-   )

ROSCOE ATES

With a stutter on his lips and a mind for comedy, Roscoe Ates became an important player in the Eddie Dean series. He remained with Dean through fifteen sidekick roles. (1895-1962)

GENE AUTRY

With five stars on the Hollywood walk of fame, Gene Autry's credits include radio, television, records, singing, movies, songwriting, and the list goes on. Fond of Autry's singing voice, Will Rogers first suggested that young Gene give radio a try. (1907-   )

BOB BAKER

It has been told that Bob Baker's mother contacted Universal Studios, which resulted in a signed contract for her son. With his horse Apache, Baker became a screen favorite and entered into the ranks of top money-making Western stars for the year 1939. (1910-1975)

SMITH BALLEW

Smith Ballew began his show business career as a radio singer. His success in radio led him to the Hollywood stages where he became a singing cowboy star. (1911-1985)

JIM BANNON

Jim Bannon is probably best known for his cinecolor series of Eagle-Lion Films where he portrayed the role of Red Ryder. Later he mainlined "The Adventures of Champion" television shows during 1955-1956. (1911-1984)

ROY BARCROFT

Hailing from Crab Orchard, Nebraska, and performing in more than 200 Westerns, Roy Barcroft is remembered as "King of the Heavies," as he battled and plotted foul deeds against the world's most celebrated cowboy heroes. (1902-1969)

DON "RED" BARRY

After struggling as a bit player, Don Barry's career was enhanced when he was given his first starring role in the 1940 Republic serial, "The Adventures of Red Ryder." From 1942-1945, he was voted as being in the top-ten money-makers in Western films. (1912-1980)

GENE BARRY

With experience in stock and Broadway musicals, Gene was television's Bat Masterson for three seasons. Turned from lawman to professional gambler, Bat Masterson travelled the West bearing his trademarks, a derby hat and a gold-tipped cane. (1921-   )

BUZZ BARTON

Buzz Barton was a great horseman and rodeo star who began his career at the age of 10, when he was skillful enough to "place in the money" for various rodeo events. The movie producers snapped him up to work in Westerns. His movie career lasted more than twelve years. (1914-1980)

GREGG BARTON

Still a rugged figure, Gregg Barton frequently appears at Western festivals. A native New Yorker, he played football at the University of North Carolina before heading for Hollywood and a career as a Western badman. Barton appeared in more than 250 television shows and played a villain in the last serial made, *Blazing the Overland Trail*, in 1956. (1912-   )

NOAH BEERY, SR.

This range rider was brother to Wallace Beery and the father of Noah Beery, Jr. Noah, Sr.'s acting career centered around villainous roles which would become his calling card. Because of his former stage experience, Beery was able to take on movie acting with ease. (1882-1946)

REX BELL

Prior to becoming Lieutenant Governor for the state of Nevada, Rex Bell rode in the saddle for the Hollywood cameras through many Western sagas. (1903-1962)

BOBBY BLAKE

A faithful companion to Red Ryder, young Bobby Blake rode alongside Allan "Rocky" Lane and "Wild" Bill Elliott. Later, he made his way into bigger pictures and television shows. (1933-   )

SALLY BLANE

During the 1930s, as a young and vibrant actress, Sally Blane shared her Western movie appearances with Hoot Gibson, Randolph Scott, and James Newill. (1910-)

DAN BLOCKER

Best known as Hoss Cartwright on the long-running television classic "Bonanza," Dan Blocker provided tenderness, strength, and comedy for the viewing enjoyment for fans of all ages. Blocker's sudden death during the 1972-73 taping season left a void that could not be filled, and the series ended shortly afterward. (1928-1972)

MONTE BLUE

Although his name may not be recognizable to many, certainly Monte Blue's face is one that Saturday afternoon buckaroos will remember as that "bad guy" hassling the cowboy hero. Early in his career, Blue was a major star in silent films. (1890-1963)

WARD BOND

Ward Bond (right) portrayed the wagon master, Major Seth Adams, who led a wagon train from Missouri to California during the 1870s in the long-running show "Wagon Train," which aired on NBC, and later on ABC. (1903-1960) Robert Horton (left) was Indian scout Flint McCullough on the series.

RICHARD BOONE

A fine actor, Richard Boone achieved major recognition with the big studios. His greatest accomplishment came on television's "Have Gun Will Travel." Boone portrayed the intelligent hired gunman, Paladin, in 226 episodes of this popular show from 1957 until 1963. (1917-1981)

ADRIAN BOOTH

Adrian Booth, aka Lorna Gray, gained her fame by playing outstanding serial villainess roles at Republic such as Vultura in *Perils of Nyoka*. Booth later co-starred in Westerns with Monte Hale, Bill Elliott, and others. (1921-   )

WILLIAM BOYD

Born in Cambridge, Ohio, William Boyd became a favorite of youngsters everywhere as he portrayed Hopalong Cassidy on television and in the movies. Wearing his solid black outfit, astride his spotless white stallion, Topper, Boyd made quite an impression wherever he appeared. (1895-1972)

LANE BRADFORD

The son of another screen badman, John Merton, rough-and-tough Lane Bradford had the face that Saturday matinee audiences loved to hate. His character drove the hero to the range to search out and capture Bradford when he got out of control. (1922-1973)

SCOTT BRADY

Born in Brooklyn, New York, this former lumberjack was the brother of actor Lawrence Tierney. Brady seemed to be right at home with any acting assignment, and he landed a television show in 1959 where he became Shotgun Slade, in the series with the same title. (1924-1985)

WALTER BRENNAN

Shown here with Dack Rambo (right) (1941-1994) from the television series "The Guns of Will Sonnett," Walter Brennan proved once again that his appearance gave something special to the production of any film or show in which he appeared. (1894-1974)

LLOYD BRIDGES

Beginning his film career as a bit character in Columbia B-Westerns, Lloyd Bridges is best remembered in A-oaters as the calculating but immature deputy to Marshal Gary Cooper in the classic *High Noon*. Bridges also starred in CBS-TV's "The Loner" for 26 half-hour shows. (1913-   )

RAND BROOKS

Rand Brooks' career was enhanced when he appeared in what many proclaim is the "best motion picture ever made," *Gone with the Wind.* B-Western fans remember him as sidekick to Hopalong Cassidy. (1918-   )

JAMES BROWN

After riding through B-Western features with the likes of Wild Bill Elliott and others, James Brown landed a starring role in 164 episodes of "The Adventures of Rin Tin Tin" from 1954-1957. (1920-1992) Lee Aaker (left) was cast as Corporal Rusty along with the German Shepherd, Rin Tin Tin.

JOHNNY MACK BROWN

Following an outstanding football career at the University of Alabama, Johnny Mack Brown ventured to Hollywood where he was quickly signed to a contract by MGM Studios. Brown was chosen to play the lead in the 1930 film *Billy the Kid* which launched his career as a Western star. (1904-1974)

YUL BRYNNER

This Russian-born, bald-headed actor became an unusual Western hero. In the film *The Magnificent Seven,* Yul Brynner was joined by fellow actors Steve McQueen, Charles Bronson, Robert Vaughn, Brad Dexter, Horst Bucholz, and James Coburn. (1915-1985)

JACK BUETEL

Jack Buetel portrayed Billy the Kid in *The Outlaw*, producer Howard Hughes's famous debut film in which Jane Russell also appeared. Buetel later delighted his fans by appearing with Edgar Buchanan in the television movie, *Judge Roy Bean* in 1956. (1915-1989)

SMILEY BURNETTE

Smiley Burnette provided sidekick companionship to Gene Autry, Roy Rogers, Sunset·Carson, Bob Livingston, and Charles Starrett. An accomplished musician (It has been told that he could play over 100 musical instruments.), Burnette wrote many Western songs, including the classic "Ridin' Down the Canyon." (1911-1967)

FRED BURNS

During his versatile acting career, Fred Burns appeared in a number of silent Western movies, dating back to the year 1916. In the mid-1920s, Burns turned to character roles including sheriff, ranch owner, and the like. (1878-1915)

PAT BUTTRAM

Cast initially as a cowboy companion to Gene Autry, Pat Buttram later landed a major role as the tight-fisted Mr. Haney on the hit television show "Green Acres." Buttram was rated by many as one of the funniest comedians around, and he was very much in demand on the after dinner speaker circuit. (1916-1994)

JAMES CAGNEY

Born in New York City, superstar James Cagney was best known for his gangster films, but he also took the time to display his talents before the Western filming crews at Warner Brothers, Paramount, and MGM Studios. Cagney's best-known Western appearance was in *The Oklahoma Kid* with friend Humphrey Bogart. (1899-1986)

58

RORY CALHOUN

In addition to his more than 40 major studio productions, Rory Calhoun landed the starring role in a top-rated television Western entitled *The Texan*. As Bill Longley, Rory produced, narrated, and starred in 80 episodes which were aired on CBS (1922-   )

ROD CAMERON

Hailing from Canada and standing 6'4" tall, Rod Cameron quickly moved into the A-Westerns where he excelled as a big budget actor. He later starred in three television series: "State Trooper," "Coronado 9," and "City Detective." Cameron was constantly being sought and was hired by more than 10 Hollywood studios during his career. (1910-1983)

60

JUDY CANOVA

Republic Pictures kept Judy Canova very busy cranking out those female hillbilly-type pictures during the 1940s and 1950s. This lady's beautiful singing voice allowed her to bounce back from her hayseed role to let the audience know she was only acting the part. (1916-1983)

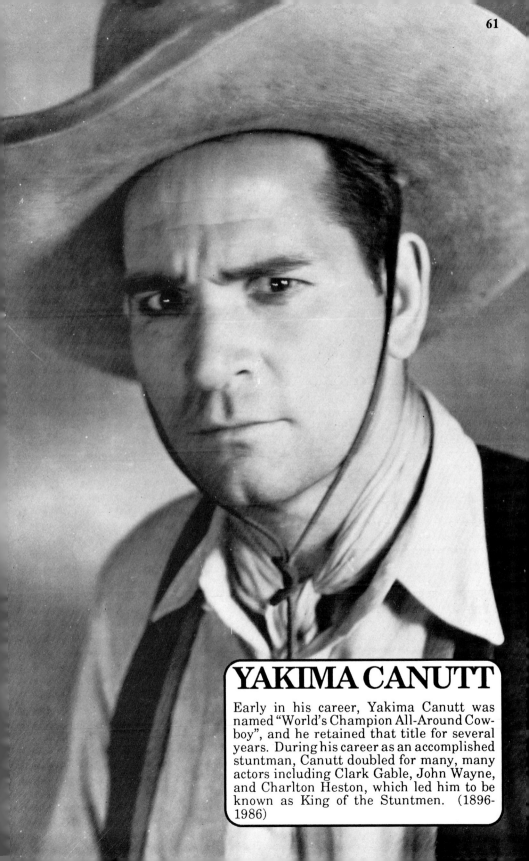

YAKIMA CANUTT

Early in his career, Yakima Canutt was named "World's Champion All-Around Cowboy", and he retained that title for several years. During his career as an accomplished stuntman, Canutt doubled for many, many actors including Clark Gable, John Wayne, and Charlton Heston, which led him to be known as King of the Stuntmen. (1896-1986)

HARRY CAREY, JR.

Still acting through the 1990s, Harry Carey, Jr. was right at home performing fine support work alongside John Wayne in Western titles including *Red River, She Wore a Yellow Ribbon, Rio Grande, Three Godfathers,* and *The Searchers.* (1921-   )

HARRY CAREY, SR.

Winner of a Golden Boot Award in 1991, Harry Carey began his film career around the year 1910. Carey continued making pictures though 1948 when his last movie, *Red River*, starring John Wayne, was released by United Artists. (1878-1947)

64

LEO CARRILLO

Cast often as a roguish, Mexican bandit, Leo Carrillo enjoyed an active movie career for almost 20 years prior to landing his famous sidekick role of Pancho in "The Cisco Kid" television series which ran from 1950-1956. (1881-1961)

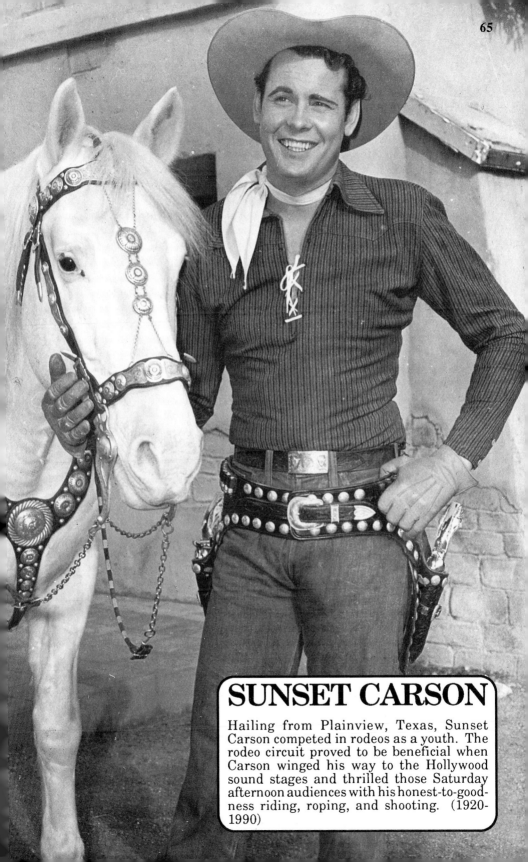

SUNSET CARSON

Hailing from Plainview, Texas, Sunset Carson competed in rodeos as a youth. The rodeo circuit proved to be beneficial when Carson winged his way to the Hollywood sound stages and thrilled those Saturday afternoon audiences with his honest-to-goodness riding, roping, and shooting. (1920-1990)

JOHN CASON

A former boxer, John Cason's Western screen appearances were numerous. He readily projected the "evil eye" which allowed the Western audience to know on which side of the law he stood. (1918-1961)

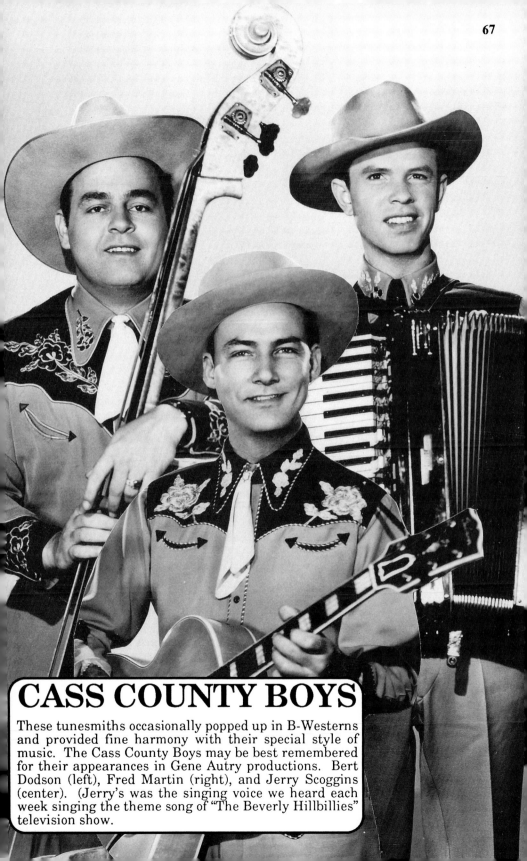

CASS COUNTY BOYS

These tunesmiths occasionally popped up in B-Westerns and provided fine harmony with their special style of music. The Cass County Boys may be best remembered for their appearances in Gene Autry productions. Bert Dodson (left), Fred Martin (right), and Jerry Scoggins (center). (Jerry's was the singing voice we heard each week singing the theme song of "The Beverly Hillbillies" television show.

ED CASSIDY

Although he held a degree in optometry, Ed Cassidy chose to become a movie actor, and it was not uncommon for him to appear in as many as 20-25 films per year. (1893-1968) Bud Osborne (left) had a career that spanned 40 years, and was an active character player in Westerns. (1884-1964)

JEFF CHANDLER

A native of Brooklyn, New York, Jeff Chandler received an Academy Award nomination for his role as Cochise in *Broken Arrow*. With fourteen starring roles to his credit, Chandler died suddenly at the age of 42. (1918-1961)

LANE CHANDLER

Losing out to Gary Cooper for stardom at
Paramount Pictures, Lane Chandler established himself as a leading man and a solid
character actor for several decades with more
than 140 screen appearances. (1899-1972)

GEORGE CHESEBRO

After eight years of bouncing around from stage to stage, George Chesebro landed into the grips of the film capital where he fell into a long-term career. Chesebro's specialty was the role of a "heavy." (1888-1959)

STEVE CLARK

Steve Clark's face was familiar to Western audiences as he played ranchers, fathers, sheriffs, and similar roles. Clark was, supposedly, employed by all the major studios. (1891-1954)

GEORGE CLEVELAND

George Cleveland's career goes back the the 19th century where he began on the stages of Broadway. He later moved to the Hollywood stages where he was known as an assorted player. Cleveland was best known as Gramps on the television show "Lassie." (1885-1957)

74

PHYLLIS COATES

Prior to receiving the leading role in Republic's 1955 serial, *Panther Girl of the Congo*, Phyllis Coates rode alongside several heroes on horseback including Whip Wilson, Johnny Mack Brown, Allan Lane, and Bill Elliott. (1927-   )

ED COBB

As a character actor, Ed Cobb appeared in more films than historians can number. During his career of nearly fifty years, Cobb was usually seen as a menace to the cowboy hero. (1892-1974)

BILL CODY

A true Western movie hero from Canada, Bill Cody portrayed his clean-living, straight-shooting image to all those matinee buckaroos who watched him on the silver screen. His son, Bill Cody, Jr. made numerous appearances with his famous father. (1891-1948)

IRON EYES CODY

His "Clean Up America" campaign brought Iron Eyes Cody worldwide fame as the Native American who got a tear in one eye while viewing unsightly litter. Cody's movie career goes back to Tom Mix, Tim McCoy, and beyond. (1904-   )

TRISTRAM COFFIN

The year 1949 was a busy one for Tris Coffin as he became part of the cast in three Republic serials. Fans will especially remember Coffin's starring role as Rocketman in the well-known and exciting serial *King of the Rocketmen*, and later as the star of television's "26 Men." (1911-1990)

CHUCK CONNORS

A former baseball star from Brooklyn, New York, Chuck Connors' athletic build and ability made him a natural for those rough-and-tough Westerns. In 168 half-hour shows, Connors portrayed Lucas McCain on the hit television program "The Rifleman." (1921-1992) Johnny Crawford, also shown here, was Chuck's co-star from the show.

ROBERT CONRAD

Alongside of co-star Ross Martin (left) (1920-1981), Robert Conrad starred in the superior CBS-Television production entitled "Wild, Wild West." The hour-long show consisted of 104 successful episodes which remained on the network from 1965-1969. (1935-   )

GARY COOPER

In 1952 Gary Cooper was honored for his screen work when was presented his second Oscar for the classic western *High Noon*. (1901-1961) Pictured alongside Cooper in a co-starring role was Grace Kelly, who later became Princess Grace of Monaco.

RAY "CRASH" CORRIGAN

When the script called for a daring person with athletic ability, Ray Corrigan filled the order. He was truly a dare-devil and considered the feats he performed a part of his daily life. Corrigan appeared in 24 episodes of the popular series The Three Mesquiteers. (1902-1976)

CAROLINA COTTON

With a delightful smile on her face, Carolina Cotton warbled and yodeled in pictures with the best stars of the saddle. Following her movie and singing career, Cotton settled in California and became a school teacher.

84

BUSTER CRABBE

Born in Oakland, California, Buster Crabbe is probably best known as Flash Gordon and Buck Rogers from those popular serials of the 1930s. Crabbe later found his place in Westerns where he appeared for more than 25 years in dozens of oaters including the Billy Carson and Billy the Kid series for PRC (1908-1983)

DICK CURTIS

Bully, boss of the riders, menace to the cowboy hero, meanest man in town—those titles could apply to Dick Curtis on the screen. It was no wonder that villain roles were readily available to Curtis, and he appeared in more than 80 features and seven serials. (1902-1952)

86

KEN CURTIS

Ken Curtis ended his career as the lovable Festus Hagen, deputy to Matt Dillon in the long-running "Gunsmoke" television show aired by CBS. Earlier in his career, Curtis was a member of the world famous Sons of the Pioneers Western singing group and starred in a string of musical Westerns. (1916-1991)

BOB CUSTER

After starring in a number of Western films, Bob Custer left the movie business in 1938 to work for the city of Los Angeles. This easy-going, hard-working, good looking actor was credited in more than 40 films during his short career. (1898-1974)

ROYAL DANO

This native New Yorker was often cast as a difficult, grumbling old-timer in rural and western settings. Royal Dano's bigger films include *King of Kings, Big Bad Mama,* and *Bend of the River.* (1922-1994)

STEVE DARRELL

It was a long trail from Steve Darrell's home state of Iowa to the gates of the Hollywood studios, but once there, he had sticking power. Darrell's smooth, easy going mannerisms complemented many pictures during his career. (1904-1970)

ART DAVIS

Art Davis credits Gene Autry with getting him into the Western movie scene. With pals Bill Boyd and Lee Powell, Davis made a string of films for PRC. (1913-1987)

GAIL DAVIS

After appearing in more than a dozen Gene Autry films, Gail Davis was given her own television series in which she portrayed Annie Oakley. Davis was also a favorite leading lady to Johnny Mack Brown, Allan Lane, Jimmy Wakely, and others. (1925-)

JIM DAVIS

A tall, tough guy who began his acting career as an outlaw type, Jim Davis developed into a leading man during the 1950s. He later achieved his greatest fame as the elder Ewing on the hit television program "Dallas." (1915-1981)

RUFE DAVIS

In the early 1940s, Rufe Davis rode along with Bob Livingston and Bob Steele and thrilled audiences as the famous Three Mesquiteers. In 1964, Davis—along with another comic, Smiley Burnette—became a part of the cast of the ever popular television show, "Petticoat Junction." (1908-1974)

EDDIE DEAN

Eddie Dean's beautiful singing voice and his likeable personality took him to the lights of the movie sound stages where he evolved into a top money-making Western star. Dean was credited for writing over 100 songs including the hits "Hillbilly Heaven" and "One Has My Name; the Other Has My Heart." (1907-   )

YVONNE DeCARLO

This Canadian-born actress was actively employed in horse operas during the late 1940s and early 1950s. Yvonne DeCarlo played a variety of roles including a fiery-tempered saloon girl, female outlaws, and glamorous women. (1922-   )

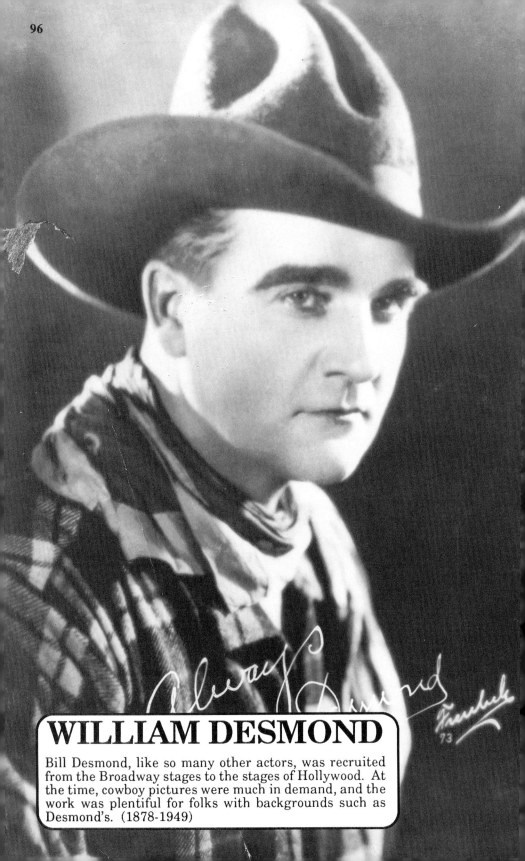

WILLIAM DESMOND

Bill Desmond, like so many other actors, was recruited from the Broadway stages to the stages of Hollywood. At the time, cowboy pictures were much in demand, and the work was plentiful for folks with backgrounds such as Desmond's. (1878-1949)

ANDY DEVINE

Andy Devine's voice shouting, "Hey, Wild Bill! Wait for me!" became the standard opening of the television show "Wild Bill Hickok," which starred Guy Madison. Prior to his stint with Madison, Devine was the sidekick pal of Roy Rogers in nine Republic Pictures productions. (1905-1977)

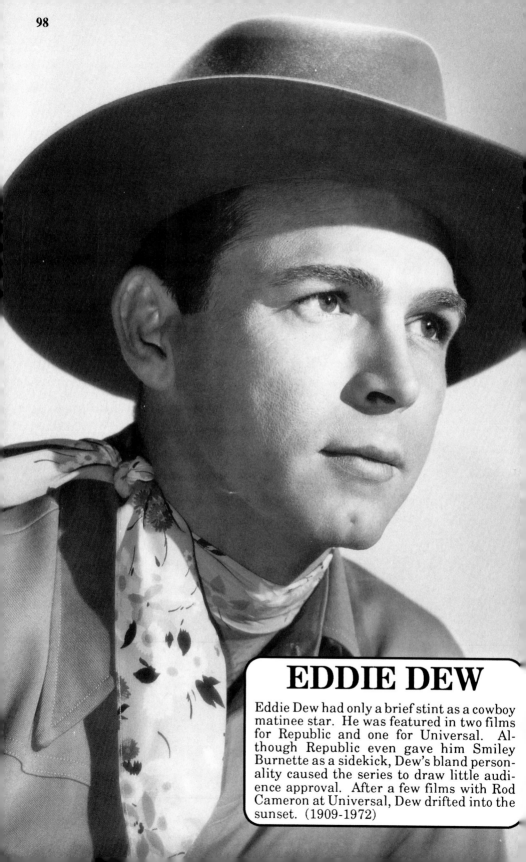

EDDIE DEW

Eddie Dew had only a brief stint as a cowboy matinee star. He was featured in two films for Republic and one for Universal. Although Republic even gave him Smiley Burnette as a sidekick, Dew's bland personality caused the series to draw little audience approval. After a few films with Rod Cameron at Universal, Dew drifted into the sunset. (1909-1972)

RICHARD DIX

With the ability to play all types of roles, Richard Dix never failed to entertain the theatre trade. Through the years, Dix's talents were welcomed at MGM, RKO, and Paramount Studios. (1893-1949)

JIMMY DODD

Jimmy Dodd went from Mesquiteer to Mouseketeer. Prior to being signed by Walt Disney to head up television's daily "Mickey Mouse Club," Jimmy Dodd teamed with Bob Steele and Tom Tyler for a number of Three Mesquiteer oaters for Republic Pictures. (1910-1964)

KIRK DOUGLAS

A major star who made numerous Western films and co-starred in many others, Kirk Douglas is best remembered for his portrayal of the modern cowboy who came afoul of the law in *Lonely Are the Brave*. Douglas was outstanding as John Wayne's semi-crooked pal in *The War Wagon* where he blended toughness and comedy with perfection. (1916-   )

JAMES DRURY

Known on the small screen for his long-running and popular portrayal of The Virginian, James Drury rode his way through 225 episodes of the television show with the same name. (1934-   )

KENNE DUNCAN

Of all the roles he played during his career, Kenne Duncan seemed to prefer the role of the heavy. Duncan appeared in more than 100 films and serials for Republic Pictures alone. (1902-1972)

DON DURANT

Don Durant (right) portrayed television's Johnny Ringo, a famous gunslinger who became sheriff during the 1880s, in the series of the same name. Mark Goddard (left) played Durant's deputy, and pretty Karen Sharpe (center), who worked at her father's general store, was Ringo's romantic interest in the series. (1932-   )

DAN DURYEA

Dan Duryea was the epitome of the smooth-talking, underhanded villain who tested the spirit of many A-Western heroes. In contrasting roles, he sided with the law in several big-budgeters of the 1950s-1960s. (1907-1968)

106

CLINT EASTWOOD

As CBS-TV introduced "Rawhide" to the viewing audience in 1959, Clint Eastwood obtained his first notable role as Rowdy Yates. He is shown here with the show's star Eric Fleming. (1924-1966) Eastwood's career has blossomed through the years, and he was awarded an Oscar for best actor for the film *Unforgiven*. (1930-   )

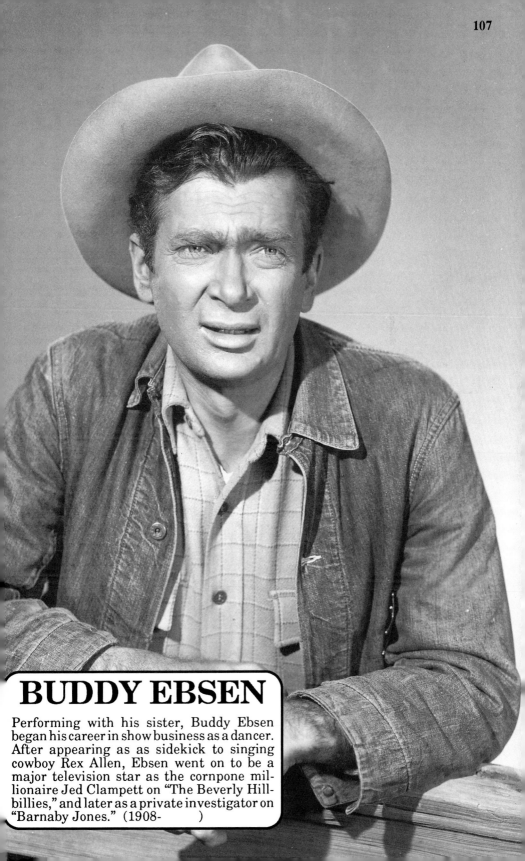

BUDDY EBSEN

Performing with his sister, Buddy Ebsen began his career in show business as a dancer. After appearing as as sidekick to singing cowboy Rex Allen, Ebsen went on to be a major television star as the cornpone millionaire Jed Clampett on "The Beverly Hillbillies," and later as a private investigator on "Barnaby Jones." (1908-   )

CLIFF EDWARDS

As the voice of Jiminy Cricket in the Walt Disney film *Pinocchio*, Cliff Edwards sang the hit song "When You Wish Upon a Star." Along the trail, Edwards' career landed him in a string of oaters with cowboy stars Charles Starrett and Tim Holt during the early 1940s. (1895-1971)

PENNY EDWARDS

Penny Edwards brought beauty to the screen as her career allowed her to stop by Republic Studios long enough to appear in a half dozen Roy Rogers pictures. Edwards also appeared in some Allan Lane and Rex Allen movies. (1929-   )

JACK ELAM

This rough-and-tough screen-stealing character actor always seemed to fit well into any western setting. In the short-lived television series "The Dakotas," Elam portrayed Deputy J. D. Smith. (1916-   )

BILL ELLIOTT

A self-proclaimed peaceable man, Bill Elliott was always prepared to battle the bad guys. Perhaps he was best known for his many portrayals of the comic book character Red Ryder and his movie nickname Wild Bill. (1905-1965)

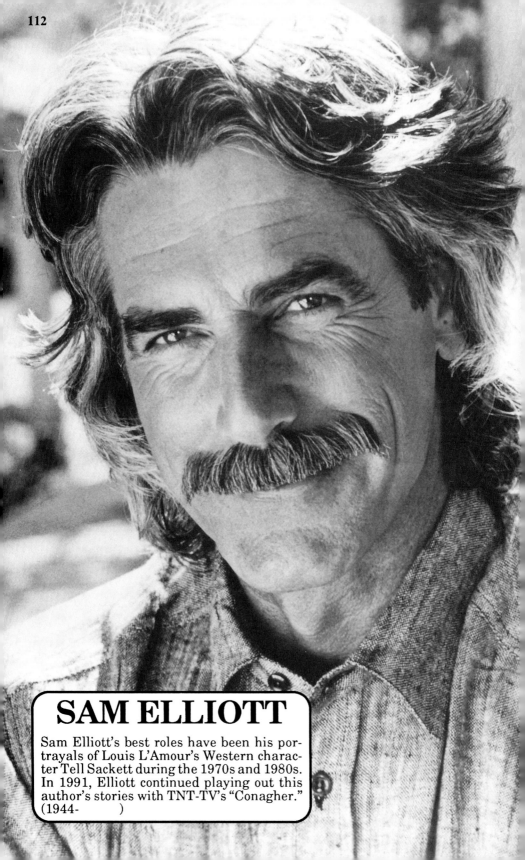

SAM ELLIOTT

Sam Elliott's best roles have been his portrayals of Louis L'Amour's Western character Tell Sackett during the 1970s and 1980s. In 1991, Elliott continued playing out this author's stories with TNT-TV's "Conagher." (1944-   )

FRANK ELLIS

Brawny and bad is an apt description of big Frank Ellis. His carer spanned some four decades, and most of that time he was a B-Western and serial badman. His forte was playing brutes and bushwackers. Ellis' ugliness, size and gruff voice made him an ideal movie henchman. (1897-1969)

JAMES ELLISON

Like so many actors in Western flicks, Jimmy Ellison became an accomplished rider as a youngster. He was selected to portray Johnny Nelson in the early productions of a new "Hopalong Cassidy" series at Paramount Pictures. Ellison later co-starred with another Cassidy sidekick, Russell Hayden, in a series for Lippert. (1910-1993)

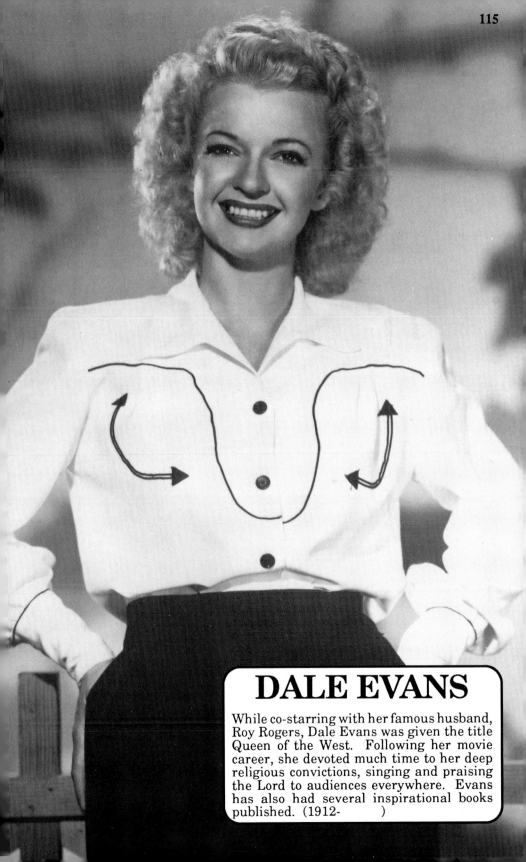

DALE EVANS

While co-starring with her famous husband, Roy Rogers, Dale Evans was given the title Queen of the West. Following her movie career, she devoted much time to her deep religious convictions, singing and praising the Lord to audiences everywhere. Evans has also had several inspirational books published. (1912-   )

GENE EVANS

Gene Evans displayed the kind of talent that kept him busy in films as a sought-after character actor. Evans appeared in numerous Westerns including *Cattle Queen of Montana, Pat Garrett & Billy the Kid, Support Your Local Sheriff, The Sacketts,* and others. (1922-   )

MURIEL EVANS

A pretty lady, Muriel Evans appears astride a beautiful horse in a scene from a Buck Jones 1936 film entitled "Silver Spurs." Evans was also a saddle gal to John Wayne, Tex Ritter and William Boyd. (1911-   )

RICHARD FARNSWORTH

A truly kind and gentle man, Richard Farnsworth was an accomplished stuntman before he demonstrated a natural acting ability. His starring role in *The Grey Fox* was superb and is easily considered his best performance. (1920-   )

TOMMY FARRELL

Tommy Farrell made his screen debut at Monogram where he was featured in six pictures with Johnny Mack Brown and six with Whip Wilson. As Corporal Carson, Farrell became a regular in the popular television series "The Adventures of Rin Tin Tin."

EVELYN FINLEY

Evelyn Finley was a superior horsewoman who acted in several low-budget Westerns for Monogram Pictures during the early 1940s. She provided excellently-staged trick riding in and out of the saddle for films like the The Range Busters' *Cowboy Commandos* in 1943. (1915-1989)

SHUG FISHER

Best remembered as the man behind the bass with The Sons of the Pioneers, the famous singing group with which he appeared in many Roy Rogers films, Shug Fisher was a comic as well as a character actor. His last feature film role was with James Garner in *The Castaway Cowboy* in 1974. (1907-1984)

ERROL FLYNN

Best known for swashbuckling roles, Errol Flynn made a number of top-notch Westerns including *They Died with their Boots On*, *Dodge City*, and *San Antonio*. (1909-1959) Olivia DeHavilland (shown here) was teamed with Flynn for ten films during her screen career.

HENRY FONDA

Henry Fonda was an excellent Broadway stage actor whose American characters have always been imbued with honesty and integrity. Fonda played mostly heroes, but also played a few villains towards the latter part of his career. His television appearances included a starring role in "The Deputy," a 30-minute television show on NBC for 76 episodes from 1959-1961. (1905-1982)

124

DICK FORAN

A movie cowboy with tremendous singing talents, Dick Foran enjoyed success as a star for Warner Brothers' B-Westerns during the mid-1930s, and then was relegated to mostly support parts for another 30 years. Foran was a top money-making Western star from 1936-1938, and was particularly good in *Land Beyond the Law* and *Empty Holsters*. (1910-1979)

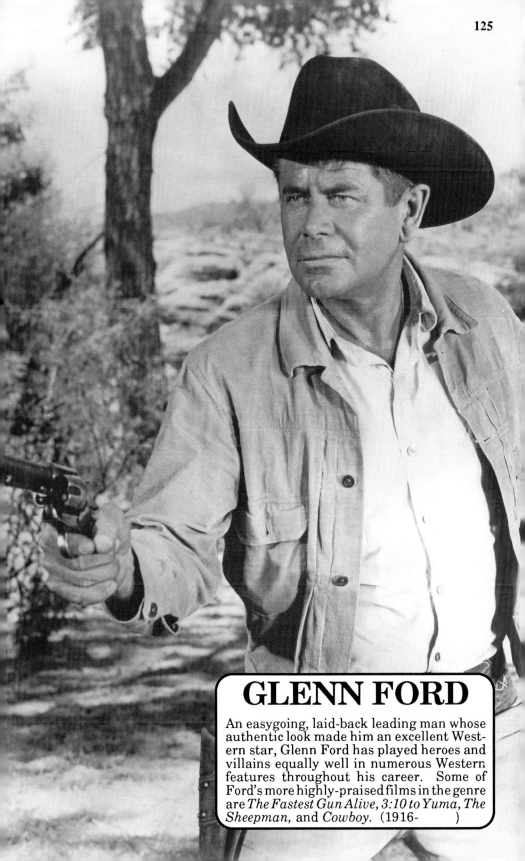

GLENN FORD

An easygoing, laid-back leading man whose authentic look made him an excellent Western star, Glenn Ford has played heroes and villains equally well in numerous Western features throughout his career. Some of Ford's more highly-praised films in the genre are *The Fastest Gun Alive*, *3:10 to Yuma*, *The Sheepman*, and *Cowboy*. (1916-   )

JANE FRAZEE

Jane Frazee's pert and sparkling personality in Universal's B-musicals proved advantageous when she signed on at Republic Pictures in the 1940s. Frazee was later teamed alongside Roy Rogers in five of his most expensive Trucolor Westerns. (1918-1985)

TERRY FROST

A Western flick without a bad guy just wouldn't fly. Terry Frost, who was truly a kind and gentle man, portrayed a real nasty villain in many of his more than 300 television and movie appearances. (1906-1993)

CLARK GABLE

Despite being remembered best as Rhett Butler in *Gone with the Wind*, Clark's first talking motion picture was a 1931 Western movie titled *The Painted Desert* with Bill Boyd. In a 1961 release, Gable ended his film career portraying an aging horse wrangler along with Marilyn Monroe in Arthur Miller's *The Misfits*. (1901-1960)

JAMES GARNER

Best known for his role as television's Maverick, James Garner climbed the acting ladder to star in several major film productions. Garner also achieved TV fame as he portrayed a hard luck private eye in the long-running series, "The Rockford Files." (1928-
)

BM-2

BUD GEARY

When Bud Geary snarled and demanded that they "hand over the money," the movie fans could see the fear come over the faces of his victims. An automobile accident in Hollywood prematurely ended his life. (1898-1946)

ED "HOOT" GIBSON

Hoot Gibson's comic touches enlivened Westerns beginning in the 1910s, and he remained active in sound films until 1960. Gibson was a top money-making Western star in 1936, and he returned to the screen during the 1940s for Monogram's thrill-a-minute series, The Trail Blazers. (1892-1962)

KIRBY GRANT

Kirby Grant's greatest popularity came as rancher Sky King in the series of the same name which aired in the 1950s. Prior to his television career, Monogram Pictures kept Grant busy as a movie cowboy for a number of their productions. (1911-1985)

LORNE GREENE

In 1959 Lorne Greene became Ben Cartright in what is known as one of television's most popular Westerns, "Bonanza." The series became second only to "Gunsmoke" for longest-running Western television series. (1910-1987)

ANNE GWYNNE

Once signed by Universal Studios in 1939, Anne Gwynne immediately was thrust into well-received company gallopers and musicals with stars including Johnny Mack Brown, Richard Arlen, and Abbott and Costello. Gwynne later appeared in the well-produced Rod Cameron A-Western *Panhandle* for United Artists in 1948. (1918-
)

KARL HACKETT

Entering film work in 1936 after departing to Hollywood from his hometown of Carthage, Missouri, Karl Hackett appeared in serials as well as Westerns. Hackett's roles were primarily those of a gang leader or henchman. (1893-1948)

LOIS HALL

Appearing in B-Western roles from the late 1940s through the early 1950s, Lois Hall did the majority of her pictures as saddle gal with Charles "Durango Kid" Starrett and Johnny Mack Brown. Hall also performed straight drama simultaneously for a number of Republic low-budgeters. (1926-   )

TY HARDIN

Ty Hardin was a hard-riding cowboy who played Bronco Lane in the Warner Brothers' television series. He kept himself in shape and became a successful and believable cowboy star. (1930-   )

JOHN HART

The Lone Ranger is probably the best Western fictional character ever created. John Hart portrayed the famous masked man in a number of episodes of the well-known television series. He also was TV's "Hawkeye" and starred in Columbia' Jack Armstrong serial. (1917-   )

NEAL HART

After obtaining an engineering degree, Neal Hart headed west where he worked a number of jobs while waiting for his break into the movie business. (1879-1949)

WILLIAM S. HART

A pioneer in the days of early Western movies, Bill Hart, along with his horse pal Fritz, rode across the silent screen to thrill the young and old at the local theatre. Ah, yes! Those were the days! (1864-1946)

RAYMOND HATTON

Everyone who loves and enjoys Western films has seen Raymond Hatton in countless productions. He was Johnny Mack Brown's sidekick in a string of films for Monogram Pictures in which Ray repeatedly reminded Brown not to call him Old Timer. (1887-1971)

RUSSELL HAYDEN

A native of California, Russell Hayden was probably best known as Hoppy's pal Lucky Jenkins, as he appeared in a number of Hopalong Cassidy pictures. Hayden later starred in the self-produced "Cowboy G-Men" television series before moving into directing and producing for his own television production company. (1912-1981)

GEORGE "GABBY" HAYES

A veteran screen actor and a true gentleman of the old school, Hayes came up through the ranks to become one of the silver screen's most beloved characters by portraying a bearded, toothless old codger with a weakness for telling tall tales. (1885-1969)

144

RITA HAYWORTH

Early in her career, under the stage name of Rita Cansino, Hayworth appeared in B-Westerns with Tom Keene, Tex Ritter, George O'Brien, and the Three Mesquiteers. (1918-1987)

VAN HEFLIN

Van Heflin was an outstanding character actor whose career eventually led him into leading roles. Perhaps his best-known portrayal was that of a nester whom Alan Ladd aided in the classic movie *Shane*. (1910-1971)

KELO HENDERSON

Fast draw expert Kelo Henderson was the perfect choice to play Arizona Ranger Clint Travis, the action star of Russell Hayden's "26 Men" TV series, filmed in Arizona. (1923-   )

CHARLTON HESTON

Besides working in epic films including *The Ten Commandments* and *Ben Hur*, Charlton Heston took the time also to star in many Westerns including *Will Penny*, *Pony Express*, and *Major Dundee*. (1923-   )

148

RILEY HILL

A versatile actor in Western pictures, Riley Hill played U.S. marshals, sidekicks, henchmen and whatever a story required. His career was most closely associated with Johnny Mack Brown and Whip Wilson between 1945 and 1953.

EARLE HODGINS

This loveable character actor is a personal favorite of the publisher and others. Earle Hodgins excelled at playing medicine show barkers, con men and characters that required a special touch which only he could provide. (1893-1964)

STERLING HOLLOWAY

Although best known for his voiceover work in Walt Disney's animated productions, Sterling Holloway's career included a stopover at Republic Studios where he appeared with Gene Autry in five saddle dramas. (1905-1992)

151

JACK HOLT

Jack Holt successfully made the move from
silent to sound film star and continued as a
character actor late in his career. The father
of B-Western star Tim Holt and cowgirl
Jennifer Holt, his hard-edge dramatics
greatly enhanced such highly-praised oaters
as *My Pal Trigger*, *The Arizona Ranger*, and
The Strawberry Roan. (1888-1951)

JENNIFER HOLT

Jennifer Holt exuded refreshing sophisti-
cated presence in numerous oaters during
the 1940s, when she was a leading lady at
Universal and PRC to popular B-movie cowboys Johnny Mack Brown, Tex Ritter, Eddie
Dean, and Lash LaRue. (1920-   )

TIM HOLT

Tim Holt was inducted into the Cowboy Hall of Fame after having a successful career in radio, television and the movies. As a top-notch cowboy star for RKO pictures, Holt earned the prestige of being a top money-making Western star. (1918-1973)

LEE HORSLEY

Lee Horsley brought his western talents to the television audience when he portrayed Ethan Allen Cord in "Paradise" which ran for a couple of years on CBS. Recently, he has been seen as television's new "Hawkeye."

GEORGE HOUSTON

George Houston was best known for his fast-paced Lone Rider series in which he and Fuzzy St. John rode to combat the bad guys of the untamed west. The Saturday matinee buckaroos sat glued to their front-row seats during those action-packed adventures. (1896-1944)

JACK HOXIE

Riding a horse was probably Jack Hoxie's best talent, as he began his stint as a movie cowboy star in 1910. In addition to making over 130 films, Hoxie also became a circus and wild west show performer and a rancher in his home state of Oklahoma. (1885-1965)

WILL HUTCHINS

While performing magic tricks on the streets of his hometown of Los Angeles, Will Hutchins quickly developed the desire to become an actor. His lucky break came as Hutchins was signed by Warner Brothers to star in the popular television series "Sugarfoot." (1932-   )

JACK INGRAM

Jack Ingram popped up in hundreds of B-Westerns and television shows during his career. Ingram also built his own movie set town where many Westerns were filmed. (1902-1969)

LOIS JANUARY

Twelve B-Westerns which were cranked out in less than three years are credited to Lois January. January's cowboy co-stars were Reb Russell, Tim McCoy, Johnny Mack Brown, Bob Steele, Bob Baker, and Fred Scott.

ANNE JEFFREYS

Her natural beauty and ability to act before the camera led Anne Jeffreys to the western movie sets of Hollywood. Between 1942 and 1948, her talents were utilized in twelve B-Westerns with Buster Crabbe, Bill Elliott, Robert Mitchum, and Randolph Scott. (1923-   )

BEN JOHNSON

Born in Pawhuska, Oklahoma, Ben Johnson has always been a favorite of fans and fellow workers alike. When awarded an Oscar for his performance in *The Last Picture Show*, Johnson responded with "It couldn't have happened to a nicer fellow!" (1920-   )

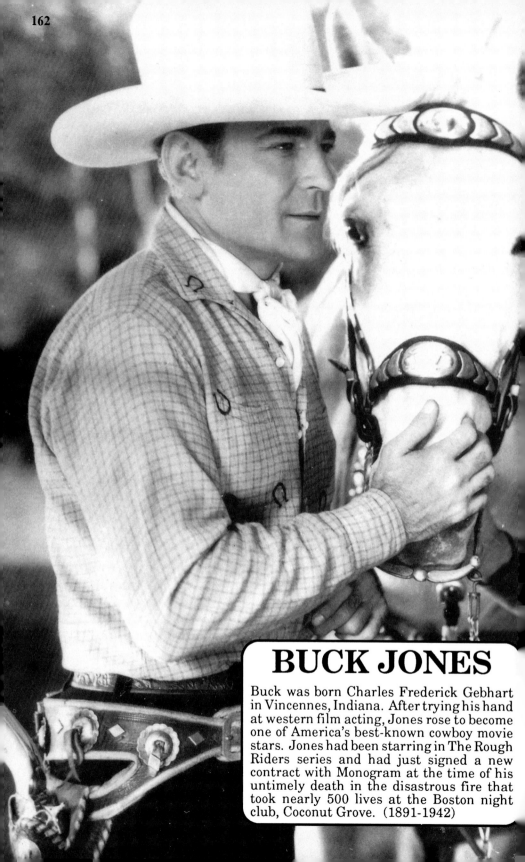

BUCK JONES

Buck was born Charles Frederick Gebhart in Vincennes, Indiana. After trying his hand at western film acting, Jones rose to become one of America's best-known cowboy movie stars. Jones had been starring in The Rough Riders series and had just signed a new contract with Monogram at the time of his untimely death in the disastrous fire that took nearly 500 lives at the Boston night club, Coconut Grove. (1891-1942)

DICK JONES

Dick hooked up with Gene Autry's Flying A Productions to be a co-star along with Jock Mahoney in "The Range Rider" television show. Jones later starred in "Buffalo Bill, Jr.," another Autry production. (1927-   )

BEVERLY JONS

Beverly Jons' short-lived career in B-Westerns lasted for only three pictures: one with Allan Lane, one with Jimmy Wakely, and one with Duncan Renaldo.

MARY ELLEN KAY

Mary Ellen Kay was a late arrival for the B-Western, but she, nevertheless, carved a niche at Republic Studios as the pretty brunette female lead in six Rex Allen oatuners from 1951-1952.

TOM KEENE

Tom Keene was seen riding and roping his way across the silver screen in many pictures during a career which spanned from 1929 until 1958. Keene was also known as the sheriff on the television western "Fury" during the late 1950s. (1896-1963)

JACK KELLY

As Bart Maverick, brother of Bret Maverick (played by James Garner), Jack Kelly acted his way through one of television's most popular shows. "Maverick" was geared to the adult audience with a humorous point of view. (1927-1992)

168

GEORGE KENNEDY

George Kennedy is well remembered for his notable roles in *Shenandoah, The Sons of Katie Elder,* and *The Good Guys and the Bad Guys.* Kennedy has also been seen more recently in The Naked Gun series with Leslie Nielsen. (1925-   )

CHARLES KING

To make his character as devious as possible, Charlie King was given names such as Blackie and The Boss. King usually sported a mustache and looked downright mean as he battled Buck Jones, Tex Ritter, Johnny Mack Brown, and others. (1895-1957)

JOHN KING

Born in Cincinnati, Ohio, John King became a member of the popular trio of Western productions, "The Range Busters." King's filming career was cut short when he was called into active duty during World War II. (1909-1987)

PEE WEE KING

Pee Wee King came from the background of
polka music which led him to form his own
Golden West Cowboys Band. King's Western movie appearances were many and provided that special musical touch to the cowboy sagas. Along with fellow musician Red
Stewart, he wrote "The Tennessee Waltz"
which is the official state song of Tennessee.
(1914-   )

FUZZY KNIGHT

A screen comic who always captured the audience's attention, Fuzzy Knight was a matinee favorite when he gave sidekick support to the cowboy star. Knight had graduated from the University of West Virginia with a law degree, but was urged to seek a career in show business. (1901-1976)

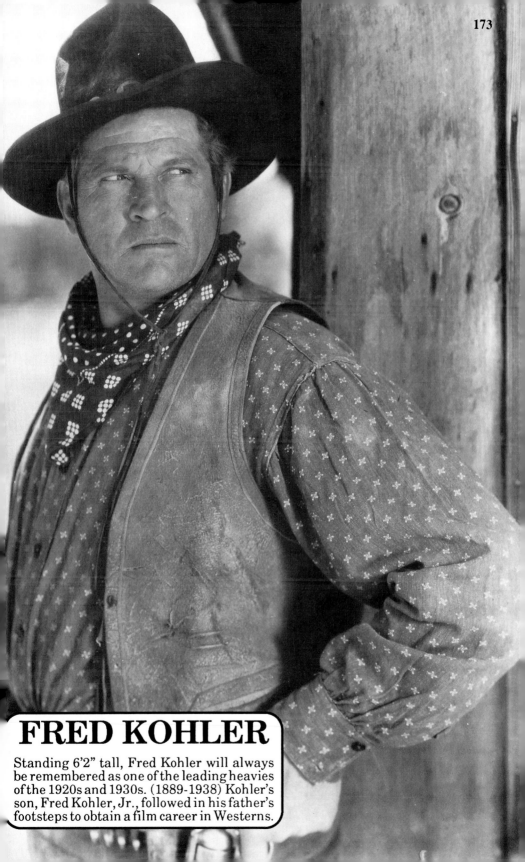

FRED KOHLER

Standing 6'2" tall, Fred Kohler will always
be remembered as one of the leading heavies
of the 1920s and 1930s. (1889-1938) Kohler's
son, Fred Kohler, Jr., followed in his father's
footsteps to obtain a film career in Westerns.

BOB KORTMAN

As a seedy, untidy-looking villain, Bob Kortman played his roles well and seemed willing to take on any assignment given to him by his screen boss. (1887-1967)

ALAN LADD

Alan Ladd starred in one of the most famous Western films of all time, the classic *Shane*. Ladd will also be remembered for his roles in *The Proud Land*, *Red Mountain*, and *Whispering Smith*. (1913-1964)

BURT LANCASTER

Although a versatile, athletic leading man who made numerous Western films, Burt Lancaster was better known as a swashbuckler than a cowboy. Some of his better pictures include *The Unforgiven, The Professionals,* and *Valdez is Coming.* (1913- 1994)

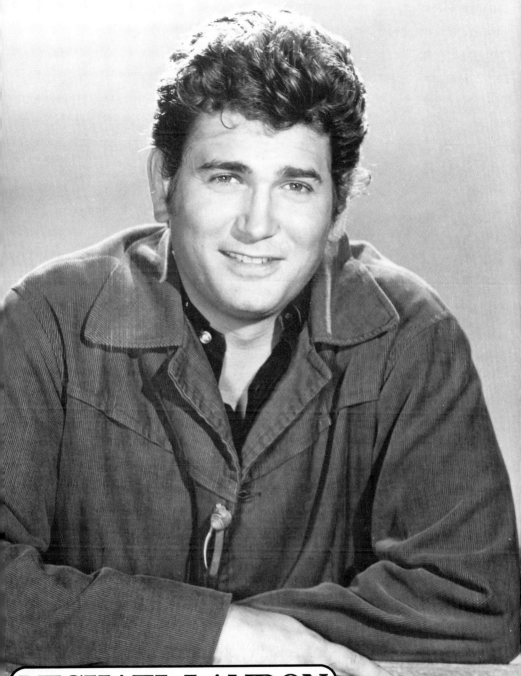

MICHAEL LANDON

Before the hit television show productions "Highway to Heaven" and "Little House on the Prairie," Michael Landon was Little Joe Cartright on the long-running "Bonanza." While still in the prime of his career, cancer of liver and pancreas took Landon's life at the age of 54. (1937-1991)

ALLAN "ROCKY" LANE

The same Rocky Lane who portrayed The Red Ryder in seven hard-riding oatburners at Republic supplied the off-camera voice for television's favorite horse, Mr. Ed, from 1961-1966. Prior to the Ryder series, Lane starred in four of Republic's finest action serials. (1909-1973)

FRANK LaRUE

Frank LaRue made the career journey from Vaudeville to the Broadway stage through the studio gates of Hollywood. LaRue's ability to be believable in almost any acting situation placed him in many horse operas. (1878-1960)

LASH LaRUE

Cracking a whip and dressed in black paved the way to B-Western stardom for Lash LaRue as he made a string of outdoor dramas for PRC and Western Adventures Productions. To the delight of Western fans across the country, Lash has been a popular guest at western film conventions for more than twenty years. (1917-   )

REX LEASE

With a smile on his face and entertaining in his heart, Rex Lease starred in a long string of horse operas and provided character support in many others. In all, Lease is credited with more than 150 Western screen appearances. (1903-1966)

MARY LEE

Mary Lee was already an accomplished singer, but still in her mid-teens when Republic placed her in a string of musical Westerns with Gene Autry. Those roles gave Lee a chance not only to warble beautifully, but also to dramatize troubled characterizations caused by domestic guardians.

GEORGE J. LEWIS

George J. Lewis was a very busy actor during the 1940s as he appeared in eighteen sound serials. The chapter play *Zorro's Black Whip* led him to a starring role alongside pretty Linda Stirling. (1903-   )

BOB LIVINGSTON

Prior to becoming a top-action Western star, Bob Livingston worked as a seaman, lumberjack, ranch hand and even a reporter for a Los Angeles newspaper. Perhaps his most notable role was that of The Lone Ranger in the Republic serial *The Lone Ranger Rides Again*. (1904-1988)

TOM LONDON

A lovable character actor, Tom London made more than 500 screen appearances along with such stars as Sunset Carson, Monte Hale, Rex Allen, Bob Steele, and almost any other cowboy you can name. (1889-1963)

ROBERT LOWERY

As a leading man during the 1940s, Robert Lowery also appeared in a dozen or more cowboy dramas. His best role came in 1949 as he was chosen to play Batman in the popular Columbia serial *Batman and Robin*. (1916-1971)

JACK LUDEN

With a mere five starring roles to his credit, Jack Luden (a member of the Luden Cough Drop family) began accepting minor parts in pictures before leaving the industry entirely in the late 1940s. (1902-1951)

JOHN LUPTON

John Lupton (right) portrayed a blood brother companion to Cochise in the TV adventure series "Broken Arrow." (1922-1993) Michael Ansara (left) was cast as the great Indian chief Cochise. (1922-1993)

PIERCE LYDEN

A veteran of countless Westerns and serials, Pierce Lyden's acting ability and skills kept him working in movie and TV Westerns for many years. (1908-   )

EMMETT LYNN

A true "old timer" character, pictured here in his distinctive baggy pants, Emmett Lynn waddled and clowned his way through many cowboy films. Lynn's last Western role was in the "Red Ryder" series with Jim Bannon. (1897-1958)

FRED MacMURRAY

As a band vocalist and musician, Fred MacMurray found his way to the sound stages of Hollywood. (1908-1991) Shown here with MacMurray is Maggie Hayes (1923-1977), his co-star in the picture *Good Day for a Hanging*, one of his fine Western portrayals.

DOUG McCLURE

Following a very active big screen career, McClure found time to get involved with TV Westerns including "The Barbary Coast," "The Virginian," and "Overland Trail." (1935-1995)

TIM McCOY

Known as Colonel Tim to millions, McCoy appeared in rodeos and Wild West shows all over the country for many years following his screen career, always projecting a good cowboy image to his fans. Tim McCoy was also a noted authority on American Indian history. (1891-1978)

JOEL McCREA

Outstanding as the strong, silent type in *Union Pacific, Ramrod,* and *Ride the High Country,* Joel McCrea became a Western star who maintained a fan following for more than 40 years. (1905-1990)

FRANCIS McDONALD

Francis McDonald established himself as a talented character actor, specializing in heavy roles as well as bit parts such as banker, rancher, sheriff, and others. (1891-1968)

LAFE McKEE

This lovable character actor's career began in 1912. Laff McKee usually portrayed the honest rancher whose daughter fell in love with the film's hero. (1872-1959)

FAY McKENZIE

After acting in only a few minor 1930s Westerns, Fay McKenzie accelerated her pace in the early 1940s with five big-budget Gene Autry pictures for Republic. McKenzie's boundless energy and genuine wholehearted rendition of several songs in *Down Mexico Way* helped give Autry what many consider to be his best picture.

STEVE McQUEEN

Steve McQueen became bounty hunter Josh Randall in the popular CBS-TV series "Wanted—Dead or Alive" for 94 half-hour episodes. Over a twenty year period, McQueen also filmed several well-received A-Westerns including *Nevada Smith*. (1930-1980)

GUY MADISON

Guy Madison was television's Wild Bill Hickock in the syndicated 30-minute show for 113 episodes. Madison's excellent physical agility for the rugged action scenes enabled him to ease into feature A-Westerns for Warner Brothers, Columbia, and Allied Artists. (1922-   )

JOCK MAHONEY

Rising from stunt double work for Charles Starrett in "The Durango Kid" series, Jock Mahoney became a television star in "The Range Rider" and, later, "Yancy Derringer." (1919-1989)

LEO MALONEY

One of the pioneers in Western flicks, Leo
Maloney made his first screen appearance
in 1914. His outdoor action pictures were
well accepted by movie goers and became big
money makers. (1888-1929)

BETH MARION

In B-Westerns for several different studios including Columbia and Universal (1935-38), Beth Marion's elegance and soft voice lent dignity whenever she was leading lady to riding heroes Buck Jones, Ken Maynard, Bob Steele Tom Tyler, Johnny Mack Brown and others. (1912-   )

DEAN MARTIN

Best known as a singer and straight man of the Martin and Lewis comedy team early in his career, Dean Martin went on to become a fine screen actor and made several Westerns including *Four for Texas, Rough Night in Jerico,* and *The Sons of Katie Elder* with John Wayne. (1917-   )

RICHARD MARTIN

Richard Martin became well known as Tim Holt's sidekick who had a continuing desire for romance. Martin's character in the series was named "Chito Jose Gonzales Bustomino Rafferty." (1917-1994) Nan Leslie (shown here) appeared in six Tim Holt productions released by RKO.

LEROY MASON

Through countless films, LeRoy Mason proved himself to be the baddest of the bad guys, playing the part of the boss in many productions. A heart attack took Mason's life while on a set at Republic Studios during the filming of *California Firebrand*. (1903-1947)

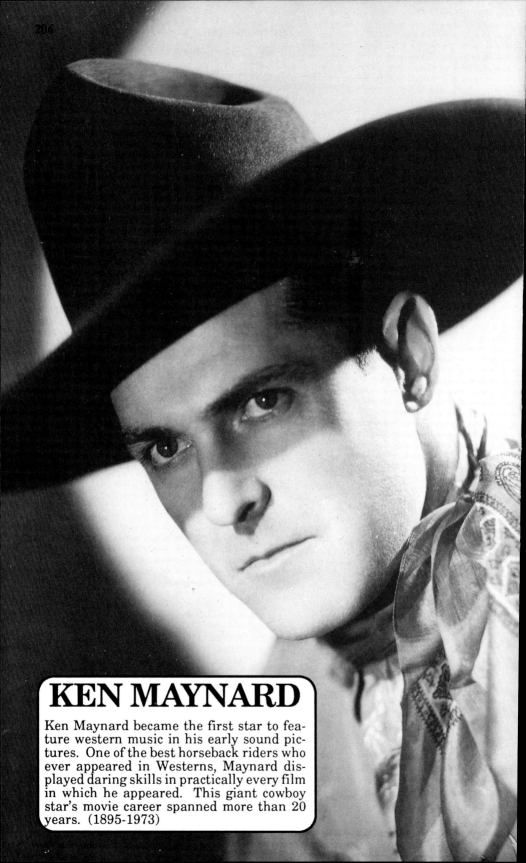

KEN MAYNARD

Ken Maynard became the first star to feature western music in his early sound pictures. One of the best horseback riders who
ever appeared in Westerns, Maynard displayed daring skills in practically every film
in which he appeared. This giant cowboy
star's movie career spanned more than 20
years. (1895-1973)

KERMIT MAYNARD

Kermit Maynard enjoyed a long-running film career that lasted more than thirty years. He could ride as well as his famous brother, Ken Maynard. (1897-1971)

VIRGINIA MAYO

A former chorus girl who gained recognition in major productions, Virginia Mayo found roles in many features including some big-budget Westerns. (1920-   )

IRIS MEREDITH

Iris Meredith acted in over 30 low-budgeters into the early 1940s and did the majority of her leading lady performances for Columbia with Charles Starrett. One of Meredith's most notable roles was her appearance in *The Taming of the West* when she stood up against Bill Elliott. (1915-1980)

LYNN MERRICK

Republic Pictures roped this honey blonde for what would eventually be 16 co-starring B-roles as she rode the range over a two-year contract period with action cowboy Don "Red" Barry. (1919-   )

BETTY MILES

A sharp-shooter as well as an outstanding horse rider, Betty Miles performed notable action scenes in B-scripts for Monogram while appearing with cowboys Tom Keene, Tex Ritter, and The Trail Blazers. Miles' character also caught the attention of Bob Steele in *Westward Bound*.

ROBERT MITCHUM

Seen as a laid-back sleepy-eyed actor, Robert Mitchum appeared in a number of Hopalong Cassidy films before rising to leading man status. Mitchum demonstrated a fantastic performance in *El Dorado* with John Wayne. (1917-   )

TOM MIX

Tom Mix was the American hero-showman of millions in silents with Selig shorts and Fox oater features through the late 1920s. During the early 1930s, he mainlined nine Universal Westerns which included the superior and highly praised *The Rider of Death Valley*. Mix closed out his film career with Mascot's 15-chapter serial *The Miracle Rider* in 1935. (1880-1940)

GEORGE MONTGOMERY

A prolific Western star who began as a stuntman, George Montgomery gave fine performances in pictures such as *The Texas Rangers*, then steered to television for 26 one-hour episodes of "Cimarron City." In recent years, Montgomery has devoted his outstanding talents to painting and sculpture. (1916-   )

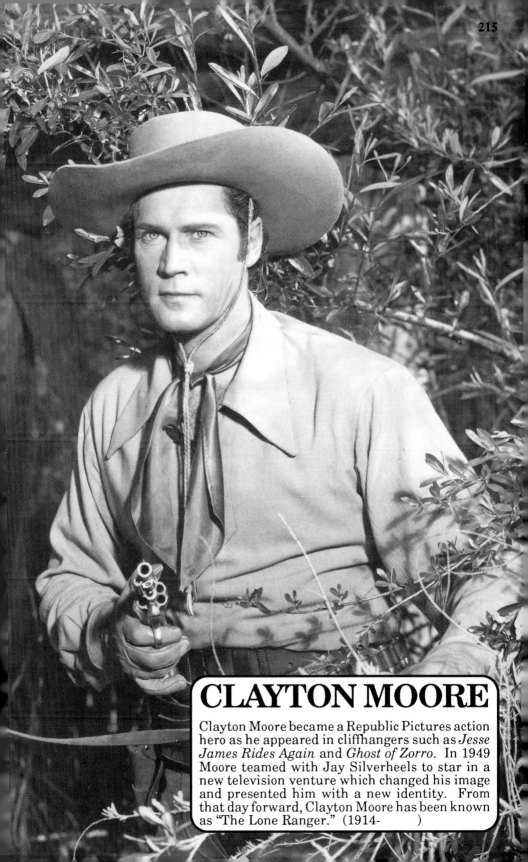

CLAYTON MOORE

Clayton Moore became a Republic Pictures action hero as he appeared in cliffhangers such as *Jesse James Rides Again* and *Ghost of Zorro*. In 1949 Moore teamed with Jay Silverheels to star in a new television venture which changed his image and presented him with a new identity. From that day forward, Clayton Moore has been known as "The Lone Ranger." (1914-   )

DENNIS MOORE

Although his face was not well known to Western movie-goers, Dennis Moore became very recognizable to audiences during his 30-year career. Moore co-starred with Linda Stirling in a top-notch chapter serial called *The Purple Monster Strikes* and also starred in the last serial ever produced, *Blazing the Overland Trail.* (1908-1964)

PETE MORRISON

Pete Morrison was known for his early silent films and his abilities as a skilled rider and stuntman. Some have said that Morrison rode a horse like he was stuck in the saddle. (1890-1973)

AUDIE MURPHY

Born in Kingston, Texas, Audie Murphy became the most decorated hero of World War II, having received 24 decorations including the Congressional Medal of Honor. With his natural, boyish features and easy-going manner, Murphy was quickly signed and starred in a number of the finest Technicolor Westerns ever released. (1924-1971)

HORACE MURPHY

It has been told that Horace Murphy appeared in over 50 Western films as well as on radio with Roy Rogers and Gene Autry. Murphy's most memorable character was that of Ananias in the Tex Ritter films. (1880-1975)

220

ZON MURRAY

Zon Murray is probably remembered only by the real Western cinema buff. He, like so many others, became type-cast as a bandit, bad guy, etc., which kept him quite busy on the cowboy movie scene. (1910-1979)

PAUL NEWMAN

This top-notch actor took time along the way of his fine films career to star and appear in a number of Westerns. Who could forget Newman's movie cowboy roles in *Butch Cassidy and the Sundance Kid, Hombre,* and *The Left-Handed Gun*? (1925-   )

HUGH O'BRIAN

Hugh O'Brian was a tough-guy leading man whose best-known role in Westerns is his character in television's "The Life and Legend of Wyatt Earp" with 226 half-hour episodes on ABC. (1925-   )

DAVE "TEX" O'BRIEN

Dave O'Brien was very active in Westerns, as he appeared and starred in more than 75 ride 'em and rope 'em films. Following his stint as an actor, O'Brien became a comedy writer for Red Skelton and received an Emmy Award for his writing skills in 1961. (1912-1969)

GEORGE O'BRIEN

In between making films, George O'Brien became a naval officer and retired as a rear admiral. Fox and RKO studios kept this muscular actor busy for almost twenty years. (1900-1985)

NELL O'DAY

Nell O'Day had expert riding abilities which so impressed Universal Pictures that the studio placed her with cowboy star Johnny Mack Brown in thirteen B-oaters. (1910-1989)

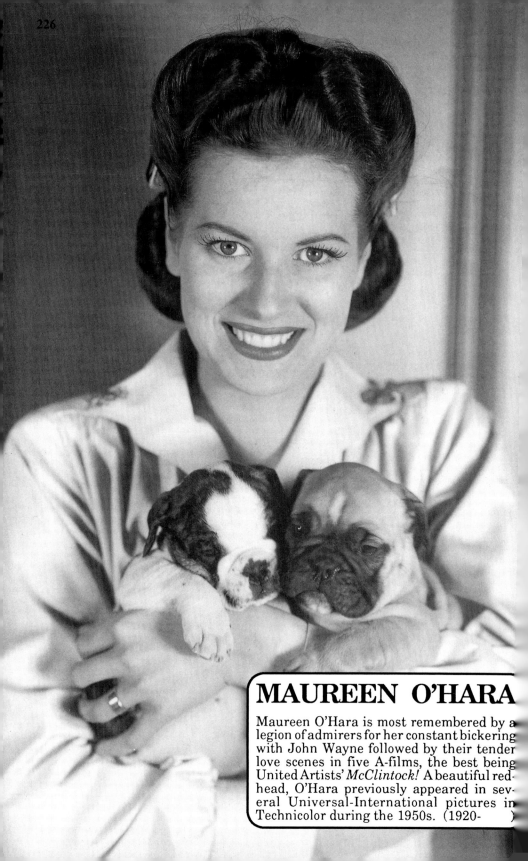

MAUREEN O'HARA

Maureen O'Hara is most remembered by a legion of admirers for her constant bickering with John Wayne followed by their tender love scenes in five A-films, the best being United Artists' *McClintock!* A beautiful red-head, O'Hara previously appeared in several Universal-International pictures in Technicolor during the 1950s. (1920-)

JACK O'SHEA

On the screen, Jack O'Shea attempted to rough up and create havoc for anyone who got in his way. On his personal appearance tours, he billed himself as Black Jack O'Shea—the villain you loved to hate! (1906-1967)

DOROTHY PAGE

This former radio entertainer-songstress came on the scene and starred in several B-Westerns including *Water Rustlers*, *Ride 'Em Cowgirl*, and *The Singing Cowgirl*. (1904-1961)

CECILIA PARKER

Cecilia Parker demonstrated reserved behavior as a leading lady in 1930s oaters for B-cowboys George O'Brien, Buck Jones, Ken Maynard, and Rex Bell. Parker's most notable scene came at the conclusion of Monogram's *Riders of Destiny* when the cute blonde happily announced that she was going to honor John Wayne's request for 100 biscuits. (1914-1993)

FESS PARKER

Walt Disney Studios snapped up Fess Parker to star in their live action productions of *Davy Crockett, King of the Wild Frontier* film. "Daniel Boone," on NBC-TV followed and placed Parker in the starring role for 165 weekly shows. (1925-   )

JOHN PAYNE

John Payne hosted 53 television episodes of "Call of the West" (reruns of "Death Valley Days") and starred in 77 episodes of "The Restless Gun." Prior to Payne's stint in television, he was cast in several big-budget musicals. Payne was also noted for his starring role in one of the best Christmas films ever made, the original *Miracle of 34th Street*. (1912-1989)

GREGORY PECK

A tall, outstanding actor, Gregory Peck made numerous fine Western films including the classic *The Gunfighter*. Peck has personally chosen his starring features, the most recent being *Old Gringo* with Jane Fonda in 1989. (1916-   )

JACK PERRIN

Jack Perrin was born in Michigan and grew up in Los Angeles where he broke into the movie business. Perrin, along with his beautiful white stallion Starlight, entertained movie goers for a 30-year span. (1896-1967)

HOUSE PETERS, JR.

The son of House Peters, the silent screen mati‑
nee idol, House Peters, Jr. was a screen heavy
who would stoop so low as to kick dogs and whip
horses in addition to robbing banks and stage
coaches. In films, Peters was brought to justice
by Roy Rogers, Gene Autry, the Cisco Kid, Jimmy
Wakely, Johnny Mack Brown, Lash LaRue, Bill
Elliott and other stars. (1916-   )

SLIM PICKENS

Banged and bruised from riding a bull as a
rodeo performer, Slim Pickens bounced into
the Hollywood scene to enjoy a long-running
role with Rex Allen. Who could ever forget
his part in *Blazing Saddles*? (1919-1983)

LEE POWELL

In 1938 a masked Lee Powell appeared as The Lone Ranger in the 15-chapter serial along with Chief Thundercloud as his faithful companion Tonto. Later, with pals Bill Boyd and Art Davis, Powell starred in a series for PRC entitled The Frontier Marshals. (1908-1944)

ELVIS PRESLEY

Although known best for his musical work, Elvis Presley starred in five Western films. His best performance was in *Flaming Star* for 20th Century Fox Studios. (1935-1977)

WAYDE PRESTON

A young Wayde Preston came on the television scene in 1957 to star in "Colt .45," a Warner Brothers Production aired by ABC-TV. (1930-1992)

JACK RANDALL

Born in San Fernando, California, the brother of movie cowboy Bob Livingston, Jack Randall became a tremendous hit with Western movie fans in his own Monogram series. Randall was blessed with a rich baritone voice which enhanced his screen performances. (1906-1945)

RONALD REAGAN

After a movie career of almost 30 years, this Hollywood actor turned the tables on his career by going into politics. Following a successful stint as governor of California, Reagan went on to become the first movie star to achieve the title of President of the United States. (1911-   )

DEPUTY
U.S.
MARSHAL

ROBERT REDFORD

Although not known primarily as a range rider, Robert Redford achieved a few starring roles in Westerns. His most notable western role is that of the Sundance Kid in *Butch Cassidy and the Sundance Kid* in which he co-starred with Paul Newman. (1937-   )

MARSHALL REED

A handsome man, Marshall Reed was able to play wherever needed—on either side of the law—in many Monogram, Eagle-Lion, and Republic films. In later life, Reed was a popular guest star at film conventions. (1917-1980)

WALTER REED

Walter Reed was once an RKO contract player
("Bombadier," Mexican Spitfire series) who
became a serial hero at Republic (*Flying Disc
Man from Mars, Government Agents vs. the
Phantom Legion*) and a screen/TV heavy
opposite Tim Holt, Annie Oakley, Clint
Walker, Rocky Lane, Randolph Scott and
others. Reed also worked in several John
Ford films. (1916-   )

BOB REEVES

Robert Jasper Reeves was born in Texas and became an expert rodeo rider, which prepared him for his Western movie career. Reeves starred in a series of silent Westerns before turning to supporting roles. (1892-1956)

DUNCAN RENALDO

Duncan Renaldo began his climb to stardom in the 1939-1940 series *The Three Mesquiteers*. He became known as The Cisco Kid in a 1945 feature film which led to a six-year portrayal of Cisco on television's "The Cisco Kid" children's show. (1904-1980)

ELAINE RILEY

This lovely lady was married to actor Rich-
ard Martin (one of Tim Holt's sidekicks).
During her busy acting career, Elaine Riley
stopped by United Artists to co-star in six
Hopalong Cassidy pictures and five other B-
Westerns.

TEX RITTER

After attending law school, Tex Ritter began his show business career by appearing in two Broadway shows before being signed by Grand National Pictures in 1936 to make a series of Western films. Ritter became well recognized when his rendition of the ballad "High Noon" won an Academy Award. His son, John Ritter, has become an accomplished actor in recent years. (1906-1974)

LEE ROBERTS

When "They went that-a-way," was yelled,
Lee Roberts, surrounded by fellow gang
members, could be seen riding fast and hard
to escape the clutches of the film's star. He
was once married to stunt lady Evelyn FInley.

PERNELL ROBERTS

In the Western field, Pernell Roberts was best known as Adam Cartright, the oldest brother on the highly-acclaimed "Bonanza" television show.

DALE ROBERTSON

A Western-type leading man who began his career in 20th Century Fox films, Dale Robertson soon moved into television with the series "Tales of Wells Fargo" for 167 episodes, followed by "Iron Horse" with 47 hour-long shows. (1923-   )

JACK ROCKWELL

Although this reliable character actor was cast most often as an honest, dependable sheriff, Jack Rockwell did switch roles occasionally to portray a businessman, rancher, or villain.

252

JIMMY ROGERS

Son of the famous entertainer/philosopher Will Rogers, Jimmy took his ranching talents through the gates of Hollywood to appear in cowboy sagas. He is best remembered as sidekick to William Boyd in the Hopalong Cassidy pictures. (1915-   )

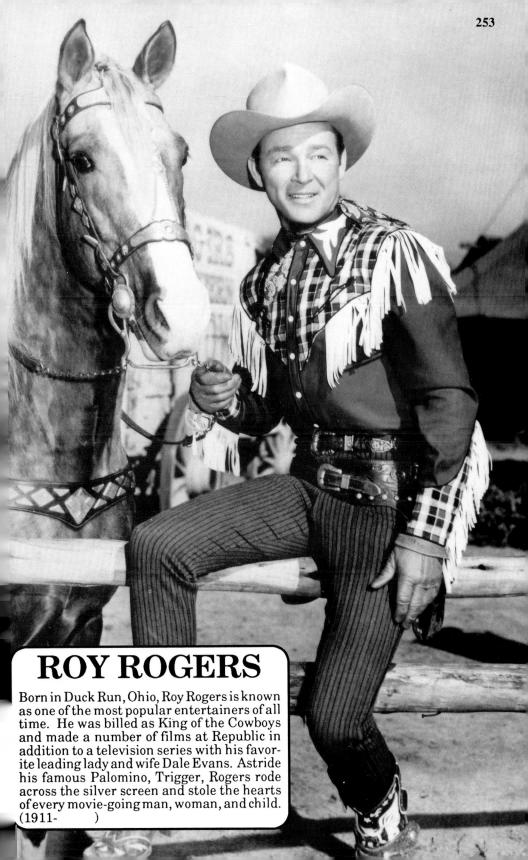

ROY ROGERS

Born in Duck Run, Ohio, Roy Rogers is known as one of the most popular entertainers of all time. He was billed as King of the Cowboys and made a number of films at Republic in addition to a television series with his favorite leading lady and wife Dale Evans. Astride his famous Palomino, Trigger, Rogers rode across the silver screen and stole the hearts of every movie-going man, woman, and child. (1911-   )

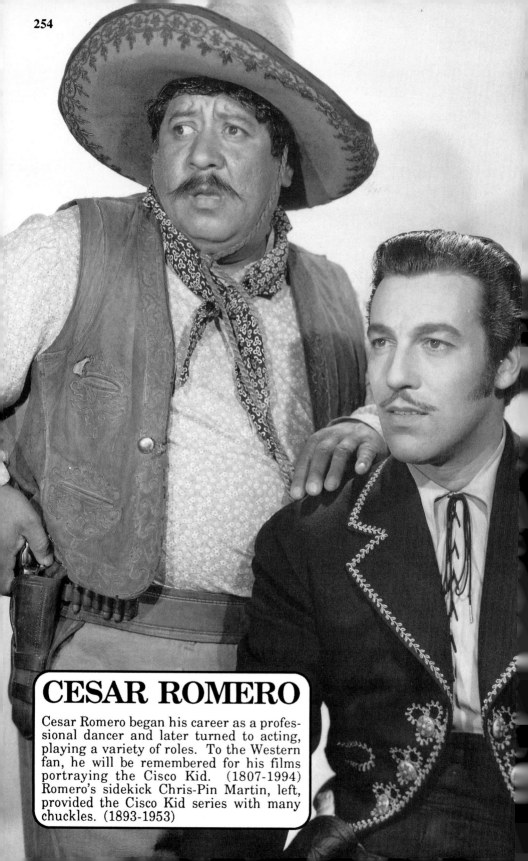

CESAR ROMERO

Cesar Romero began his career as a professional dancer and later turned to acting, playing a variety of roles. To the Western fan, he will be remembered for his films portraying the Cisco Kid. (1807-1994) Romero's sidekick Chris-Pin Martin, left, provided the Cisco Kid series with many chuckles. (1893-1953)

BUDDY ROOSEVELT

Buddy Roosevelt said, "You take what you can get if you want to break into the movie business." And that is just what he did. During his 40-year career, Roosevelt appeared as a star, bit player, stuntman, extra, and any other role he could obtain. (1898-1973)

JANE RUSSELL

Jane Russell got the attention of the movie-going public with her debut performance in Howard Hawks' controversial film *The Outlaw*. In 1948, Russell was cast with Bob Hope in a Western comedy, *The Paleface*, and in the sequel *Son of Paleface* in 1952. (1921-   )

JOHN RUSSELL

With actor Peter Brown (right), John Russell starred as Marshal Dan Troop in a Warner Brothers TV Western entitled "Lawman" which premiered in October 1958. (1921-1991)

REB RUSSELL

Before retiring from the movie business to live the life of a prominent rancher, Reb Russell turned out ten features during 1934-1935. (1905-1978)

SYD SAYLOR

Syd Saylor's face is well remembered by cowboy movie fans as he provided comic relief for the heroes in the many films in which he appeared. (1895-1962)

FRED SCOTT

Fred Scott was the strong-voiced singing troubadour with a series of low-budget Spectrum pictures during the late 1930s. During later years, Scott succeeded with a successful real estate career in California. (1902-1991)

RANDOLPH SCOTT

After leaving his hometown of Charlotte, North Carolina, while waiting for his break into movies, Randolph Scott shared an apartment and living expenses with another young actor, Archibald Leach, who later became famous as Cary Grant. Scott's friendly and gracious manner made him one of the most pupular and well-liked stars in American screen history. (1898-1987)

DAVE SHARPE

They called him Daredevil Dave because of his abilities to perform almost any stunt asked of him. Dave Sharpe doubled for almost all of the male stars at Republic and enjoyed a successful on-screen career as a serial and Western star. (1911-1979)

CAL SHRUM

While on a national tour, Cal Shrum, along with his Rhythm Rangers, was hired for an Autry film, *The Old Barn Dance*. Following that film, Shrum was in and out of Hollywood for more than ten years before moving into radio as a permanent fixture. (1910-) Alta Lee, his wife for many years, was Shrum's leading lady in films.

JAY SILVERHEELS

A full-blooded Mohawk Indian, Jay Silverheels' greatest popularity was reached when he was cast as Tonto on the long-running television program, "The Lone Ranger." (1919-1980)

THE SONS OF THE PIONEERS

In 1934 Roy Rogers and Bob Nolan teamed with Tim Spencer and Karl Farr to form this famous International musical Western group. The Sons of the Pioneers' renditions of "Cool Water" and "Tumbling Tumbleweeds" have become American cowboy standards. Left to right: Hugh Farr (1903-1980), Pat Brady (1914-1972), Bob Nolan (1908-1980), Karl Farr (1909-1961), Lloyd Perryman (1917-1977); and center: Tim Spencer (1908-1974).

LOUISE STANLEY

In low-budget oaters for five years, Louise Stanley had a regal beauty which temporarily sidetracked saddlers Tex Ritter, Bob Steele, Jack Randall, Jim Newill, and Dave O'Brien from ever wanting to lasso outlaws. (1915-1982)

BARBARA STANWYCK

An all-time great dramatic actress during Hollywood's "Golden Age," Barbara Stanwyck proved herself to be adept for outdoor action whenever hitting the saddle with A-Westerns. Later, she starred on television's "Big Valley." (1907-1990)

CHARLES STARRETT

Charles Starrett (also known as the Durango Kid) was known and respected for the 131 pictures he made for Columbia Studios. With action films enhanced by super stuntmen, such as Jock Mahoney, Starrett's films were some of the most successful ever made. (1903-1986)

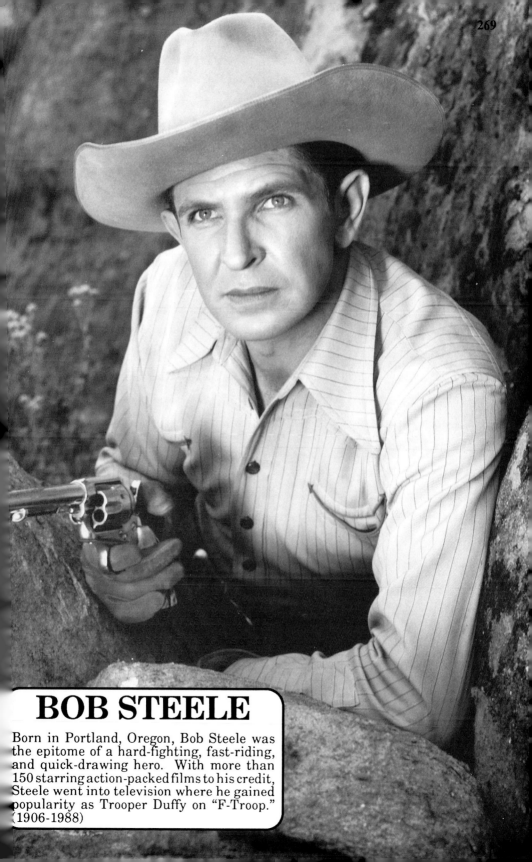

BOB STEELE

Born in Portland, Oregon, Bob Steele was the epitome of a hard-fighting, fast-riding, and quick-drawing hero. With more than 150 starring action-packed films to his credit, Steele went into television where he gained popularity as Trooper Duffy on "F-Troop." (1906-1988)

CHARLES STEVENS

Specializing in sneaky, villainous roles, Charles Stevens' film career began in 1915 in D.W. Griffith's *Birth of a Nation.* (1893-1964)

JAMES STEWART

One of the great film actors of all time whose versatility in roles is unmatched, James Stewart began to make Westerns during the 1950s. Among Stewart's many fine Western films is the classic *Winchester '73*, and the superb features *The Naked Spur*, *The Man from Laramie*, and *The Man Who Shot Liberty Valance*. (1908-   )

PEGGY STEWART

A highly popular leading lady at Republic, Peggy Stewart's presence graced numerous fast-moving B-gallopers starring Sunset Carson, Bill Elliott, and Allan Lane. An excellent rider, Stewart was able to overcome some rough dunking in well water from studio badman Roy Barcroft during the chapterplay *Son of Zorro* in 1947. (1923-   )

LINDA STIRLING

Although a former beauty model, Linda Stirling began rigorous acting in Republic's thrilling 1944 serial *The Tiger Woman*, and interspersed more action cliffhangers with studio Westerns. (1921-   )

AL "FUZZY" ST. JOHN

Before becoming a sidekick to Lash LaRue, Buster Crabbe, George Houston, and others, Fuzzy St. John teamed with his uncle, Roscoe (Fatty) Arbuckle and Buster Keaton to make a series of comedy shorts. (1892-1963)

JUNE STOREY

A very attractive and pert blonde, June Storey became Gene Autry's female co-star in ten of the singing cowboy's popular Republic musicals during the 1939-1940 period. (1918-1991)

GLENN STRANGE

As a singer, this rugged, mustached actor performed Western songs on the radio which led him into Western films. Away from the western scene, Glenn Strange was cast in three films as the Frankenstein monster. In 1962, Strange joined the "Gunsmoke" television show as Sam, the bartender, a role which he portrayed until his death. (1899-1973)

BARRY SULLIVAN

Barry Sullivan was the leading man-type who took time out from feature films to persue an active television career. Along with co-star Clu Gulager (right), Sullivan portrayed Pat Garrett in "The Tall Man" television programs. (1912-1994)

HELEN TALBOT

Helen Talbot's B-Western film career was short-lived, as she appeared in only ten pictures from 1943-1944 and 1955. Talbot's leading men included Don Barry, Roy Rogers, Allan Lane, and Bill Elliott.

LYLE TALBOT

As a teenage magician, Lyle Talbot worked his way into acting by portraying heavies and accepting character roles. Talbot worked frequently in cliffhangers including *Batman and Robin, Atom Man vs. Superman,* and *Chick Carter, Detective.* (1902-   )

HAL TALIAFERRO

One of the busiest Western actors in Hollywood, Hal Taliaferro did his part to keep the attention of the audience. Many times he was cast as an unshaven, grimy character. Taliaferro was also known as Wally Wales, due to a career name change along the way. (1895-1980)

DUB TAYLOR

Dub "Cannonball" Taylor enjoyed a long career playing sidekick to six Western stars between 1939 and 1950. In later life, Taylor was a welcomed member of the country music/comedy TV show "Hee Haw." (1907-1994)

ROBERT TAYLOR

A handsome leading man, Robert Taylor portrayed Billy the Kid in the MGM production of the same title. Taylor later became host of television's "Death Valley Days." (1911-1969)

5097-54

MAX TERHUNE

A master showman, Max Terhune entertained thousands with his feats of magic, ventriloquism, impersonations, and comedy. Terhune's movie career began in 1936 when he appeared with Gene Autry in *Ride, Ranger, Ride*. Later, he rode with the Three Mesquiteers and the Range Busters. (1891-1973)

RUTH TERRY

A lively and vivacious singer/dancer with
Republic through the mid-1940s, Ruth Terry
appeared in many fast-paced musicals, comedies, and dramas, in addition to four Roy
Rogers pictures. (1919-   )

FRED THOMSON

A true action star who knew what his audience wanted, Fred Thomson, along with his famous horse Silver King, kept the moviegoers coming back to see more. (1890-1928)

TOM TYLER

From silent films to the sound era, Tom Tyler was a box-office draw for more than twenty years. Tyler made thirteen films as a member of Republic's "Three Mesquiteers." (1903-1954)

LEE VAN CLEEF

Lee Van Cleef's screen credits are many
including two with film favorite Clint
Eastwood. Van Cleef became a leading man
in European Westerns and was cast in the
classic *High Noon*. (1925-1989)

DALE VAN SICKEL

Dale Van Sickel excelled as a stuntman and heavy. At the end of a typical Western picture, when the outlaws were rounded up and slapped in the calaboose, one could be pretty sure that Dale Van Sickel would be in the group of villains. (1907-1977)

WALLY VERNON

Best known as a comic sidekick to Don "Red" Barry and Allan Lane, this former broadway song and dance man left the B-Westerns after a brief stay. Wally Vernon left his mark in saddlers as a most unusual sidekick character. (1904-1970)

JIMMY WAKELY

Rated as one of the better singers of his day, Jimmy Wakely landed a film contract with Monogram to star in his own series. One of Wakely's best recording efforts was a Christmas duet with Margaret Whiting, entitled "Silverbells." (1914-1982)

CLINT WALKER

A huge man in stature, Clint Walker is best remembered for his long-running television series "Cheyenne." The show ran for 107 hour-long episodes. (1927-   )

EDDY WALLER

Eddy Waller arrived in Hollywood in 1936 and enjoyed an active career as a character actor through the 1950s. In the Allan "Rocky" Lane series, Waller played an old coot by the name of Nugget Clark. (1889-1977)

JOHN WAYNE

Born in Winterset, Iowa, "Duke's" often-used expression, "That'll be the day," in the 1956 film *The Searchers*, inspired Buddy Holly to write his number-one hit using the same catch-phrase as its title. Internationally known and a super box-office attraction, Wayne starred in Westerns, serials, comedies, dramas, war pictures and action films for nearly forty years. (1907-1979)

DENNIS WEAVER

Dennis Weaver (left) (1924-   ) along with "Gunsmoke" buddies Amanda Blake and Milburn Stone, provided a top-notch cast which supported the show's star James Arness who portrayed the famous Marshal Matt Dillon.

RAQUEL WELCH

A mainstay with several 20th Century-Fox features during the late 1960s, Raquel Welch's only movie Westerns on the A-plane have been *Bandolero!* and *100 Rifles*. (1940-
)

DAN WHITE

In the make-believe world of B-Westerns, the hero knew to watch the cattle and put an extra guard on the stagecoach's strong box when Dan White's character rode across the screen. (1890-1973)

LEE "LASSES" WHITE

Lee "Lasses" White supplied comedy and sidekick assistance to Jimmy Wakely in twelve hay-burners for Monogram Pictures during the 1940s. White loved the West and enjoyed being a part of the Western films. (1888-1949)

RAY WHITLEY

Give him a horse, a rope, and a six-gun, and
Ray Whitley was right at home; give him a
guitar and he would warble some smooth
Western sounds. Whitley wrote "Back in the
Saddle Again" and sold it to Gene Autry.
(1901-1979)

CHARLES "SLIM" WHITTAKER

This badman's character enhanced every screen appearance. Whittaker was cast as a ranch hand, deputy, stagecoach driver, and wherever he was needed. His film career career ended in the late 1940s after more than 30 years in cowboy pictures. (1893-1960)

BOB WILKE

Bob Wilke's career began as a Hollywood stuntman and evolved into a steady acting involvement. Western film fans will recall Wilke's appearance in the classic *High Noon*. (1913-1989)

BILL WILLIAMS

"The Adventures of Kit Carson," with 104 half-hour segments, kept Bill Williams (1915-1992) busy maintaining law and order. Williams appeared in the series along with Mexican sidekick El Toro, played by Don Diamond. (1916-1992)

GUINN "BIG BOY" WILLIAMS

A rough-and-tough happy-go-lucky cowpoke, Guinn "Big Boy" Williams starred in his own series for two years, and then concentrated on giving supporting roles, usually as a sidekick companion to others including Errol Flynn, Ken Curtis, Roy Rogers. (1900-1962)

TEX WILLIAMS

A one time vocalist with Spade Cooley's Orchestra he later formed his own group, The Western Caravan. Tex Williams became a major recording star and was featured in a series of Western shorts for Universal-International. (1917-1985)

CHILL WILLS

A well-known face and unforgettable voice, Chill Wills portrayed the crooner in the Laurel & Hardy film *Way Out West*, and he also supplied the voice of Francis the talking mule. (1902-1978)

305

JAY WILSEY

He was born with the handle of Jay C. Wilsey, but for screen purposes, he was known as Buffalo Bill, Jr. His first starring role was an action Western, *Rarin' to Go*, produced in 1924. (1896-1961)

WHIP WILSON

Whip Wilson's ability to wield a bullwhip led him to a movie contract with Monogram Studios as a top Western hero. With grizzly-faced Andy Clyde (right) as his sidekick, Wilson became a memorable celluloid range rider. (1915-1964)

MARIE WINDSOR

This cinema lovely, cast as the lead character in the 1952 film *Outlaw Women*, also appeared with Bill Elliott, George Montgomery, and others. In 1959 Windsor signed on to co-star with Scott Brady for 78 television episodes of "Shotgun Slade." (1922-   )

JOAN WOODBURY

All good B-Westerns had a very important place for the cowgirl, and Joan Woodbury rode alongside some of the best: Hopalong Cassidy, Tex Ritter, Tim McCoy, Roy Rogers, Johnny Mack Brown, and Bob Steele. In 1945 Woodbury acquired the lead role in *Brenda Star, Reporter*, a 13-chapter serial for Columbia. (1915-1989)

HARRY WOODS

Harry Woods looked the part of the big boss of the outlaw riders, a role he portrayed often. Woods' movie acting career spanned forty years prior to his retirement in 1961. (1889-1968)

HANK WORDEN

John Wayne took a liking to this loveable character and included Hank Worden in many of his productions including *True Grit*, *McClintock*, *The Alamo*, and *The Searchers*. (1901-1992)

JANE WYATT

With Western film titles including *Hurricane Smith*, *Buckskin Frontier*, and *Canadian Pacific*, the talented Jane Wyatt was very much at home on the range. (1911-   )

TONY YOUNG

Known only as Cord, Tony Young lived up to the television show's title "Gunslinger." An expert with a six-gun, Young portrayed an undercover agent for the Army. The show had a short run of only twelve episodes in 1961.

LET'S
NOT
FORGET

The following pages contain a listing of 264 additional names of actors whom we also wish to remember. These talented individuals have contributed much to the history of Western films. Athough we have made every effort to "round-up" the majority of the Western players, we hope all readers understand that it would be impossible for us to list them all in one book.

Eddie Acuff	Lon Chaney, Jr.	Martin Garralaga
Betty "Julie" Adams	Michael Chapin	Leo Gordon
Jane "Poni" Adams	Tom Chatterton	Fred Graham
John Agar	Betty Compson	James Griffith
Richard Alexander	Tex Cooper	Dorothy Gulliver
Lona Andre	Benny Corbett	William Haade
Richard Arlen	Don Costello	Herman Hack
Earl Askam	Richard Cramer	Reed Hadley
Hooper Atchley	Broderick Crawford	Don Haggerty
Irving Bacon	Louise Currie	Frank Hagney
Holly Bane	Frankie Darro	Jonathan Hale
Don Barclay	John Dehner	Thurston Hall
Joan Barclay	Art Dillard	William Halop
Trevor Bardette	Jeff Donnell	John Hamilton
Robert Barrat	John Doucette	Mary Hart(aka Lynne Roberts)
Sammy Baugh	Don Douglas	Don Harvey
Warner Baxter	Douglas Dumbrille	Harry Harvey
Alfonso Bedoya	Earl Dwire	Paul Harvey
Noah Beery, Jr.	George Eldredge	Myron Healey
Hank Bell	John Elliott	Buzzy Henry
Ray Bennett	Leif Erickson	Weldon Heyburn
Lyle Bettger	Virginia Brown Faire	Doris Hill
Clem Bevens	Franklyn Farnum	Robert Homans
Robert Bice	William Farnum	Arthur Hunnicut
William Bishop	William Fawcett	Reed Howes
Stanley Blystone	Dorothy Fay	Olin Howlin
Bill "Cowboy Rambler" Boyd	Frank Fenton	Al Hoxie
Truman Bradley	Al Ferguson	Wesley Hudman
Neville Brand	Elinor Field	Kay Hughes
Peter Breck	Richard Fiske	Maurita Hugo
Mary Brian	Robert Fiske	Paul Hurst
Al Bridge	Paul Fix	Lloyd Ingram
Herman Brix	Alice Fleming	Frank Jacquet
Steve Brodie	Tex Fletcher	John James
Reno Brown	Sam Flint	Art Jarrett
Lucille Browne	Byron Folger	Si Jenks
Edgar Buchanan	Francis Ford	Chubby Johnson
Bob Burns	Carol Forman	I. Stanford Jolly
Budd Buster	Preston Foster	Gordon Jones
Rocky Camron	Douglas Fowley	Victor Jory
Mary Jane Carey	Olin Francis	Ian Keith
Jean Carmen	Billy Franey	Cy Kendall
Horace Carpenter	Robert Frazer	Robert Kent
John Carroll	Clem Fuller	John Kimbrough
Wheaton Chambers	June Gale	Jack Kirk

Fred Kohler, Jr.
Frank Lackteen
Ethan Laidlaw
Jack Lambert
Eddie Laughton
Harry Lauter
George Lloyd
Arthur Loft
Wallace MacDonald
Ian MacDonald
Kenneth MacDonald
J. Farrell MacDonald
Betty Mack
Cactus Mack
Helen Mack
Barton MacLane
Murdock MacQuarie
Frank McCarroll
Patti McCarty
Merrill McCormack
Philo McCullough
J. P. McGowan
Joe McGuinn
Christine McIntire
John McIntire
Rory Mallinson
Ted Mapes
Chris Pin Martin
Frankie Marvin
Carl Matthews
Lew Meehan
Blanche MeHaffey
John Merton
Gertrude Messinger
Charles Middleton
Ray Middleton
Walter Miller
Frank Mitchell
Art Mix
Ruth Mix
Montie Montana
Dickie Moore
Milburn Morante
Lee Morgan

George Morrell
Wayne Morris
Tom Neal
James Newill
Eva Novak
Wheeler Oakman
Sarah Padden
Jack Padjan
Ted Palmer
Eddie Parker
Shirley Patterson
Sally Payne
Leonard Penn
Ralph Peters
Lee Phelps
Ed Piel
James Pierce
Snub Pollard
Hal Price
Stanley Price
Hugh Prosser
Denver Pyle
Dorothy Revier
Don Kay Reynolds
Marjorie Reynolds
Frank Rice
Addison Richards
Warner Richmond
Bill "Skeeter" Robbins
Frances Robinson
Claire Rochelle
Estelia Rodriguez
Gilbert Roland
Ann Rutherford
Shelia Ryan
Marion Sais
Tom Santschi
Joe Sawyer
Billie Seward
Harry Shannon
Marion Shilling
Dorothy Short
Walt Shrum

Russell Simpson
Arthur Space
Tom Steele
Eleanor Stewart
Carl Stockdale
Harry Strang
Joe "Tadpole" Strauch
Gene Stutenroth
Forrest Taylor
Ray Teal
Don Terry
Shelia Terry
Tex Terry
Jim Thorpe
Chief Thunder-Cloud
Forrest Tucker
Minerva Urecal
Guy Usher
Virginia Vale
Emmet Vogan
Ray Walker
Luana Walters
Anthony Warde
James Warren
Pierre Watkin
Minor Watson
Martha Wentworth
Wally West
Blackie Whiteford
Stuart Whitman
Richard Widmark
Guy Wilkerson
Guy Williams
Matson Williams
Roger Williams
Foy Willing
Norman Willis
Clarence Wilson
Grant Winters
Britt Wood
Harry Worth
Frank Yaconelli
Carleton Young

NEIL SUMMERS

Stuntmen are a special breed of athlete, and they perform feats of daring few persons would attempt. One of Hollywood's top stuntmen is Neil Summers. He has also been a stunt co-ordinator on many films, and is currently branching out into character acting, co-starring in a syndicated Western series called "Lucky Luke," which is currently a big hit all over Europe, South America and the Far East. Summers has been very lucky in his chosen and dangerous profession. He is still going strong after thirty years of working in hundreds of Western movies and television series.

AFTERWORD
by Neil Summers

Now that you've gone through *The Round-Up* and seen all the grand and familiar faces staring back at you, it probably brings back many fond memories. I know it does for me. I have been a life-long Western devotee and never get tired of viewing or reading about my heroes and heroines. Even the horses and majestic locations brighten up my day! As a youngster growing up in South Africa, I spent countless hours watching Roy, Gene, Monte, Tex, Sunset, Wild Bill, Durango, Lash and all the other guys we are so enamored with, ripping across that screen, bustin' a cap on the bad guys. I knew at that time that I wanted to be a part of it all. After my family moved to the States, and I graduated from high school, I got my chance. An Audie Murphy film called *Arizona Raiders* was filming a few miles from my home in Phoenix, Arizona. While working on this film, I was able to obtain my Screen Actors Guild membership and shortly thereafter, I moved to Hollywood and was accepted into the Stuntman's Association of Motion Pictures. For the past thirty years I have been living my dream of being part of the motion picture business.

In those thirty years of being an actor, stuntman and stunt co-ordinator, I have worked with most of the great stars and directors and even got to work with Roy Rogers on a couple episodes of "The Fall Guy" television series in which Roy had guest appearances. I did five films with the great John Wayne and Westerns with Steve McQueen, Robert Taylor, Audie Murphy, Burt Lancaster, William Holden, Richard Widmark, Dale Robertson, Glenn Ford, Dean Martin, Robert Mitchum, Clint Walker, Clint Eastwood, Brian Keith, Kenny Rogers, Terence Hill, Henry Fonda, and almost any other star connected with Westerns. I have worked on many of the classic television series including "Gunsmoke," "Bonanza," "The High Chaparral," "Daniel Boone," "Cimarron Strip," "Bearcats," "How the West Was Won," "Brisco County Jr.," and hundreds more. Through my work in the Western field of films and television, I have been privileged to meet and know many of the always reliable character actors, including Tris Coffin, Dub Taylor, Don Haggerty, I. Stanford Jolley, Lane Bradford, Davey Sharpe, Tom Steele, Marshall Reed, Gene Evans, Jack Elam, Morgan Woodward, L. Q. Jones, and Strother Martin, going back into the heydays of our treasured B-Westerns.

As time marches on, and so many of our screen and personal friends leave us, books like *The Round-Up* become even more important to us and to the history of Westerns. It is collectors like myself, Clint Brown,. and Stanley Martin, along with publishers like Don Key, Roger Crowley, and Boyd Magers who preserve the legacy these fabulous cowboys and cowgirls have left us. It is an important legacy indeed, and the older I get the more I find myself wishing for those golden days of Westerns again. There are many grown men, including myself, who were guided to stay on the right path because of the men and women who are profiled in *The Round-Up*. Because I have had the opportunity to be personal friends with Charles Starrett, Dick Jones, Pat Buttram, Bob Steele, and many others, and because of a special man named Monte Hale, who is always, always gracious to his fans, I have never been disappointed in my adulation of the cowboys.

Neil Summers
Studio City, California
August 1995

SELECTED BIBLIOGRAPHY

Adams, Les, and Buck Rainey. *Shoot 'Em Ups.* New Rochelle, New York: Arlington House, 1978.

Corneau, Ernest N. *The Hall of Fame of Western Film Stars.* North Quincy, Massachusetts: The Christopher Publishing House, 1969.

Everson, William K. *The Bad Guys.* New York: Cadillac Publishing Co., Inc., 1964.

Halliwell, Leslie. *The Filmgoers Companion.* New York: Avon Books, 1970.

Jackson, Ronald. *Classic TV Westerns.* New York: Carol Publishing Group, 1994.

Jarvis, Everett G. *Final Curtain.* New York: Carol Publishing Group, 1992.

LuKanic, Steven A. *Film Actors Guide.* Los Angeles: Lone Eagle Publishing Co., 1991.

Maltin, Leonard. *Leonard Maltin's Movie Encyclopedia.* New York: Penguin Books, 1994.

Mathis, Jack. *Republic Confidential: Volume 2 — The Players.* Barrington, Illinois: Jack Mathis Advertising, 1992.

McClure, Arthur F., and Ken D. Jones. *Heroes, Heavies and Sagebrush.* Canbury, New Jersey: A. S. Barnes and Company, 1972.

Miller, Lee O. *The Great Cowboy Stars.* New York: Arlington House Publishers, 1979.

Rainey, Buck. *Those Fabulous Serial Heroines.* Metuchen, New Jersey and London: Scarecrow Press, 1990.

Rothel, David. *Those Great Cowboy Sidekicks.* Metuchen, New Jersey: Scarecrow Press, 1984.

Rutherford, John A., and Richard B. Smith, III. *More Cowboy Shooting Stars.* Madison, North Carolina: Empire Publishing, Inc., 1992.

Stewart, William T., Arthur F. McClure, and Ken D. Jones. *International Film Necrology.* New York and London: Garland Publishing, Inc., 1981.

Summers, Neil. *The First Official TV Western Book.* Vienna, West Virginia: Old West Shop Publishing, 1987.

Thornton, Chuck, and David Rothel. *Allan "Rocky" Lane: Republic's Action Ace.* Madison, North Carolina: Empire Publishing, Inc., 1990.

Towell, Garv, and Wayne E. Keates. *Saddle Pals.* Madison, North Carolina: Empire Publishing, Inc., 1994.

Turner, Steve, and Edgar M. Wyatt. *Saddle Gals.* Madison, North Carolina: Empire Publishing, Inc., 1995.

Weiss, Ken, and Ed Goodgold. *To Be Continued.* New York: Crown Publishers, Inc., 1972.

Other Movie / TV Books Available from Empire Publishing:

100 Best Films of the Century by Barry Norman
1001 Toughest TV Trivia Questions of All Time by Vincent Terrace
Allan "Rocky" Lane, Republic's Action Ace by Chuck Thornton and David Rothel
America on the Rerun by David Story
An Ambush of Ghosts by David Rothel
Bad Guys by Williams K. Everson
Candid Cowboys, Vols. 1 & 2 by Neil Summers
Classic TV Westerns by Ronald Jackson
Classics of the Gangster Film by Robert Bookbinder
Classics of the Horror Film by Williams K. Everson
Complete Films of Bela Lugosi by Richard Bojarski
Complete Films of Bette Davis by Gene Ringgold
Complete Films of Cary Grant by Donald Deschner
Complete Films of Cecil B. DeMille by Gene Ringgold and DeWitt Bodeen
Complete Films of Charlie Chaplin by Gerald D. McDonald
Complete Films of Clark Gable by Gabe Essoe
Complete Films of Edward G. Robinson by Alvin H. Marill
Complete Films of Erroll Flynn by Tony Thomas, et al
Complete Films of Frank Capra by Victor Scherle & William Turner Levy
Complete Films of Gary Cooper by Homer Dickens
Complete Films of Henry Fonda by Tony Thomas
Complete Films of Ingrid Bergman by Lawrence J. Quirk
Complete Films of James Cagney by Homer C. Dickens
Complete Films of Jeanette MacDonald and Nelson Eddy by Philip Castanza
Complete Films of Joan Crawford by Lawrence J. Quirk
Complete Films of John Huston by John McCarty
Complete Films of John Wayne by Mark Ricci, et al
Complete Films of Judy Garland by Joe Morella and Edward Z. Epstein
Complete Films of Laurel & Hardy by William K. Everson
Complete Films of Mae West by Jon Tuska
Complete Films of Marilyn Monroe by Michael Conway and Mark Ricci
Complete Films of Marlene Dietrich by Homer Dickens
Complete Films of Orson Wells by James Howard
Complete Films of Rita Hayworth by Gene Ringgold
Complete Films of Spencer Tracy by Donald Deschner
Complete Films of Steve McQueen by Casey St. Chamez
Complete Films of the Marx Brothers by Allen Eyles
Complete Films of W. C. Fields by Donald Deschner
Complete Films of William Holden by Lawrence J. Quirk
Complete Films of William Powell by Lawrence J. Quirk
Curly by Joan Howard Maurer
Don Miller's Hollywood Corral by Smith & Hulse
Early Classics of the Foreign Film by Parker Tyler
Feature Players: The Stories Behind the Faces, Vol. 2 by Jim & Tom Goldrup
Film Flubs by Bill Givens
Films and Career of Elvis by Steven Zmijewsky and Boris Zmijewski
Films Flubs, The Sequel by Bill Givens
Films of Alan Ladd by Marilyn Henry and Ron DeSourdis
Films of Alfred Hitchcock by Robert A. Harris and Michael S. Lasky
Films of Arnold Schwarzenegger by John L. Flynn
Films of Brigitte Bardot by Crawley
Films of Carole Lombard by Fred W. Ott
Films of Charles Bronson by Jerry Vermilye
Films of Clint Eastwood by Boris Zmijewsky and Lee Pfeiffer
Films of Dustin Hoffman by Douglas Brode
Films of Elizabeth Taylor by Jerry Vermilye and Aldo Vigano
Films of Frank Sinatra by Gene Ringgold and Clifford McCarty
Films of Gina Lollobrigida by Maurizio Ponzi
Films of Gloria Swanson by Lawrence J. Quirk
Films of Gregory Peck by John Griggs
Films of Greta Garbo by Conway et al

Films of Hopalong Cassidy by Francis M. Nevins, Jr.
Films of Jack Nicholson by Douglas Brode
Films of Jane Fonda by George Hadley-Garcia
Films of Katharine Hepburn by Homer Dickens
Films of Kirk Douglas by Tony Thomas
Films of Lauren Bacall by Lawrence J. Quirk
Films of Laurence Olivier by Margaret Morley
Films of Marlon Brando by Tony Thomas
Films of Norma Shearer by Jack Jacobs and Myron Braum
Films of Olivia DeHavilland by Tony Thomas
Films of Paul Newman by Lawrence J. Quirk
Films of Peter Lorre by Stephen D. Youngkin, James Bigwood, and Raymond Cabana,
Films of Robert DeNiro by Douglas Brode
Films of Robert Redford by James Spada
Films of Sean Connery by Lee Pfeiffer and Phillip Lisa
Films of Shirley MacLaine by Christopher Paul Denis
Films of Shirley Temple by Robert Windeler
Films of the Bowery Boys by David Hayes and Brent Walker
Films of the Eighties by Douglas Brode
Films of the Forties by Tony Thomas
Films of the Seventies by Robert Bookbinder
Films of the Sixties by Douglas Brode
Films of the Thirties by Jerry Vermilye
Films of the Twenties by Jerry Vermilye
Films of Warren Beatty by Lawrence Quirk
Films of Woody Allen by Douglas Brode
Final Curtain: Deaths of Noted Movie & TV Personalities
Gene Autry Reference-Trivia-Scrapbook by David Rothel
Hollywood Musical by Tony Thomas
Hollywood Western by William K. Everson
James Dean: Behind the Scene by Adams & Burns, ed.
Joel McCrea, Riding the High Country by Tony Thomas
John Wayne Scrapbook by Lee Pfeiffer
King Cowboy: Tom Mix and the Movies by Robert S. Birchard
Life & Films of Buck Jones: The SIlent Era by Buck Rainey
Life & Films of Buck Jones: The Sound Era by Buck Rainey
Moe Howard & the Three Stooges by Moe Howard
More Character People by Arthur F. McClure, Alfred E. Twomey, & Ken Jones
More Cowboy Shooting Stars by John A. Rutherford and Richard B. Smith, III
Official Andy Griffith Show Scrapbook by Lee Pfeiffer
Official John Wayne Reference Book by Charles John Kieskalt
Official TV Western Book, Vols. 2,3, & 4 by Neil Summers
Randolph Scott / A Film Biography by Jefferson Brim Crow, III
Republic Confidential: Volume 2 - The Players by Jack Mathis
Roy Rogers Reference-Trivia-Scrapbook by David Rothel
Saddle Gals by Steve Turner & Edgar M. Wyatt
Saddle Pals by Gary Towell and Wayne E. Keates
Second Feature by John Cocchi
The Cowboy and the Kid by J. Brim Crow III and Jack H. Smith
The Dick Powell Story by Tony Thomas
The Real Bob Steele and a Man Called Brad by Bob Nareau
They Sang! They Danced! They Romanced! by John Springer
This is Hollyood by Ken Schessler
Those Fabulous Serial Heroines by Buck Rainey
Those Great Cowboy Sidekicks by David Rothel
Three Stooges Scrapbook by Jeff Lenburg, Joan Howard Maurer, Greg Lenburg
Tim Holt by David Rothel
Tom Mix Book by M. G. "Bud" Norris
Tom Mix Highlights by Andy Woytowch
West That Never Was by Tony Thomas
Western Films of John Ford by J. A. Place
Whatever Happened to Randolph Scott? by C. H. Scott
Many more titles available. Send for complete list: Empire, Box 717, Madison, NC 27025